Heather Luke's
CURTAINS

CREATIVE PUBLISHING international

CHANHASSEN, MINNESOTA

www.creativepub.com

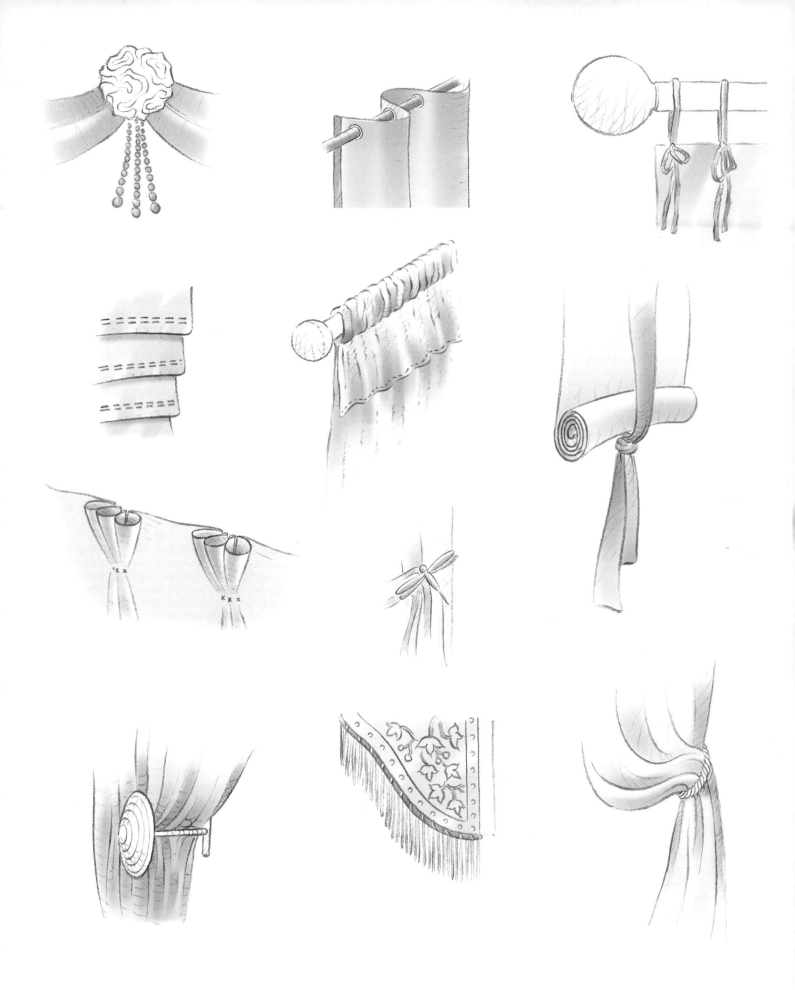

Heather Luke's
CURTAINS

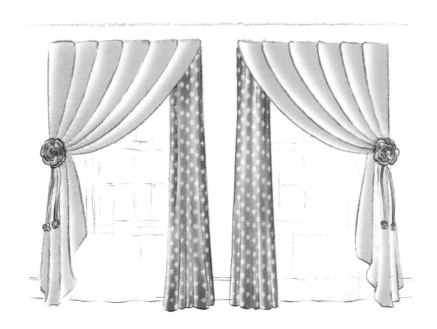

First published in the United States and Canada in 2003 by
Creative Publishing international, Inc.

18705 Lake Drive East
Chanhassen, Minnesota 55317
www.creativepub.com

Published in 2003 by
New Holland Publishers (UK) Ltd
London · Cape Town · Sydney · Auckland

ISBN 1-58923-088-4

Designer · Sara Kidd
Illustrator · Stephen Dew
Concept illustrations · Rowan Suenson-Taylor
Production · Hazel Kirkman
Editorial Direction · Rosemary Wilkinson

10 9 8 7 6 5 4 3 2 1

Reproduction by Modern Age Repro, Hong Kong
Printed and bound in Singapore by
Tien Wah Press (PTE) Ltd

Contents

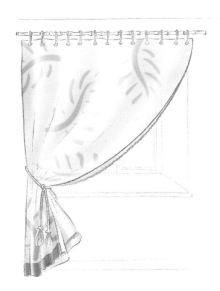

Introduction

All design from overall concept to the minutest detail depends on a series of calculated choices. The guiding principles of tradition and architecture are supplemented by personal experience of travel and previous homes and topped by the new ideas and insights of contemporary designers.

The architecture of your house is the starting point, the style of the window and its position in the house will decide the relative importance of the curtains. The shape and size will suggest suitable styles of curtaining. Whether the treatment will be contemporary or traditional will depend largely on your choice of furnishing in general, your age, experience and budget.

It does not follow that only important windows can have grand curtaining any more than an insignificant window should be ignored. The opposite is often the case. A clean, simple curtain will show off intricate architectural detail, just as a dramatic curtain can transform a boring window into an eye-catching feature.

Each window should provide some sort of visual reward. Any curtaining should be complementary to the outside view as well as to the interior style, whether a glorious vista needs little interruption or whether the curtain itself must become the focus. Consider the house as a whole, each room and therefore each window with its own identity, unfolding as you move around the house.

Fashion plays a hugely important role in every aspect of our lives and not least when it comes to our window treatments. The new fabric collections and latest ideas for curtain fittings are as much a response to the work of our leading interior designers as high street clothes are the timely reflections and dilutions of the best of the couture collections.

The spate of highly influential, and controversial, television make-over programs has made it impossible for anyone to ignore the potential for interior design and furnishings. So much so that a huge do-it-yourself market has grown up around us to furnish these aspirations. Today anything is possible.

The revolution in curtain hardware is perhaps the most striking. Ten years ago white plastic tracks were the norm and metal poles were virtually unheard of. What needed to be specially commissioned from a friendly blacksmith is now sold at every DIY and department store. A meager selection of paints has developed into a full palette and range of products to cover any surface, including metal and plastic.

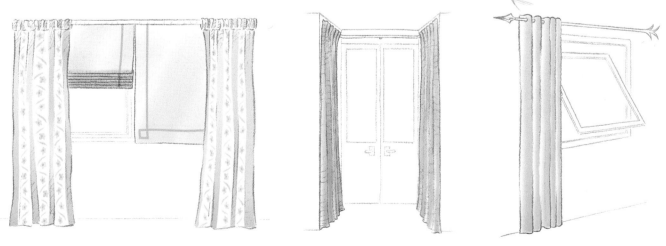

If you want something different, unusual or historical, persevere with antique markets where you will find good wooden and brass poles with real age and patina. Or, for a more contemporary approach, Check out designers' catalogues, where you will find poles in glass, acrylic, hand-stitched leather and any possible finish and color you can think of. If you still can't find what you want, commission it from a local smith or joinery workshop.

Fabric choice is very personal and although influenced by the fashion of the moment, historically correct prints and weaves, together with basic wools, cottons and linens are always available alongside the new collections. Whether you buy from the markets, from a top designer or indeed both, personal preference, budget and appropriateness are all-important.

Apart from some notation, I have deliberately avoided any specific direction for fabrics. Suggestion of plain, pattern, stripe or check is just that and may not be relevant to your situation. Design and color aren't important beyond working with your overall plan; the weight of the fabric must be right, however. There are many excellent interiors magazines that you can refer to for immediate inspiration and sourcing once you have chosen the specific curtain treatment.

The best investment you can make is to choose good quality fabric and simplicity of design for curtains, which will move from home to home with you. Then you can introduce regular changes and add life-enhancing fashion details in the accessories to keep your home up-to-date and alive.

If you are going to make your own curtains, stay within your limitation. There is no point in slaving over complicated curtains if you are going to hate the work and despair at the result. You can do a lot with blankets, throws, bedcovers, lengths of suede and other non-sew fabrics. If someone else is making them for you, enlist their help with the fabric choice and make sure that all of the details and possibilities have been discussed fully.

The first section of the book takes the window style as the starting point for choosing the curtain treatment, the second looks at different curtain designs. In reality almost all of the ideas can be translated to suit almost all of the windows, apart from the more difficult windows shown in the third section. Take a photograph of your window and copy it to the size of the sketch you are interested in. You will soon be able to see whether it is immediately possible or how it might be changed for your window.

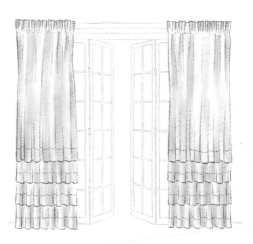

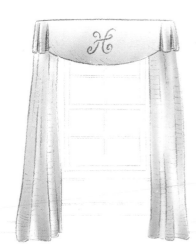

WINDOW STYLES

Three-sided Bay Windows

Some bay windows are simple casements, however, the sash window is the most common design used internationally. They almost always look out over the lawn or garden, so bear in mind the style and colors of the landscape when choosing the decoration for the room.

Always consider the bay window as a whole and very much as one with the rest of the room. Color and pattern should flow around the room, avoid treating the bay as some sort of extra feature.

▲ For a stylish, contemporary edge: a fixed pole and eyelet headings allows the curtains to pull right back.

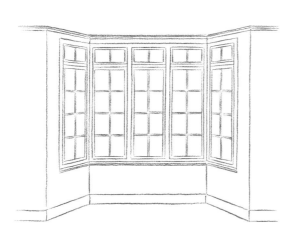

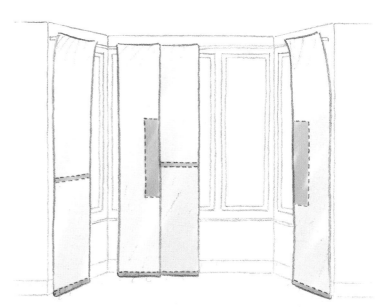

▲ Multi tracks allow a series of flat panels to be pulled around as required.

▲Where there is more wall space than window at the sides, some sort of dress curtain will be needed to keep the balance and proportion.

▲Gathered or pencil-pleated curtain headings over a metal pole are the simplest possible curtaining around a bay window.
The deep border plays on the proportions of the window.

▲Easy to fit, wide, flat rods designed for bay windows hold a fixed heading in place. Good where there is plenty of light in the room already, to lower the eye if the windows are tall, and where light can be directed lower into the room.

▲Long swags and tails suit large, elegant drawing rooms or bedrooms in period houses.

Square Bay Windows

Square bays, with either doors or windows, might be a part of the original architecture but are often the result of an extension or alteration. Those which are original will usually be of sympathetic proportion and not difficult to curtain. Those added later may be a bit too deep, too narrow, rather tall and thin, or even too wide.

Keeping the bay the same color as the rest of the room goes a long way to help an awkward bay to belong, especially for deep and narrow or "boxy" bays.

Choose curtains or blinds to soften a hard shape and to blend in with the surroundings. Any sort of blind can be fitted—as long as there is enough space in the corners to keep the blinds apart.

Curtains are most easily fitted from tracks or cornices boards. Poles can be custom-made but may be expensive.

▲ Panels on crane rods can be stored against the side, where there is blank wall, or pulled right away, where there are windows on the sides.

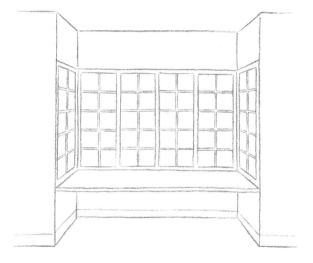

▶ Long curtains make an awkward shape softer and more elegant.

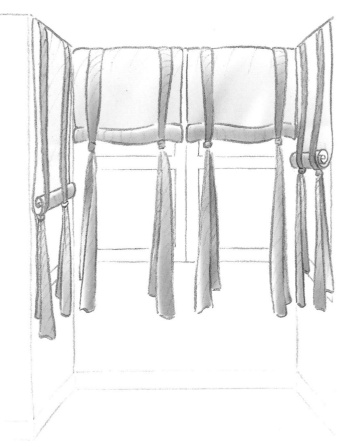

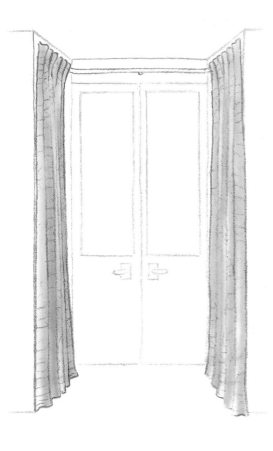

▲Decorative blinds disguise the boxiness and draw the eye beyond the window to the outside. Keep blinds and walls the same color to enhance the visual space.

▲Narrow corridors can be uncomfortable—curtains or flat panels against the sides soften and create a much more welcoming area.

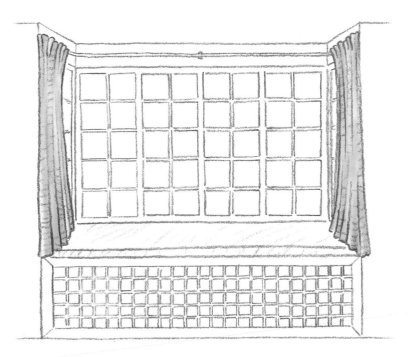

◂Boxing in below the sill provides a cozy seating area, at the same time providing useful storage beneath the seat, as bookshelves, or a radiator cover.

Five-sided Bays and Oriel Windows

Choose whether to have two or four main curtains, under-curtains or blinds, cornices or poles, by the style of the room. Poles must fit exactly and therefore may need to be custom-made. Choose a pole style which will allow the curtains to pull past the brackets. Bow windows, which are in essence curved bays, will not take blinds. Use curtains as for any other full bay or oriel window. Poles or tracks must be bent to fit and any cornice boards must be custom-made.

▲Two curtains allow maximum light to enter—important for low-ceilinged rooms. Cornices should always be designed to fit the window arrangement.

▲A small track fitted close to the frame holds the under-curtain. Heavy outer curtains need a substantial wooden pole.

▲Four curtains keep visual height and can be tied back to allow maximum light. Plan the scale and depth of any top treatments with the proportion and style of the windows.

◄ Flat panels can be moved across to filter light or stored back at the sides. At least two and possibly three tracks or poles will be needed.

Oriel windows: Always sited to make the most of a special outlook, such as a long view to the sea, or out over the countryside, or onto a garden or park. Not always the most attractive windows from the inside, long curtains are desirable to frame the sides and add height. Whatever window treatment is chosen, the overriding consideration is to frame the view beyond.

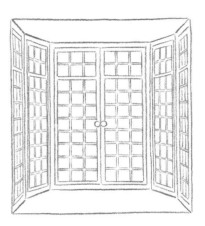

▲ Curtains across the window will cut out the bay shape, shades against the windows allow the space to be used and seen as much as is wanted.

▲ Dressing the window with drapery frames the window, allowing the view to be the focal point.

Sash Windows

Always well proportioned, sash windows are also almost always in balance with the rest of the room. Most window treatments will work, from neat formal shades to flowing drapes to traditional swags and tails. Curtains should be long. Occasionally sash windows still have their original shutters, which may be used instead of curtains but even if you do want curtains, the shutters are still useful for security and to keep out drafts.

▲ You need to be able to pull curtains back from a small window to allow maximum light. A valance fixed at ceiling height keeps the balance.

▲ Curtains hook back to allow maximum light; a shade covers the window, leaving the radiator free.

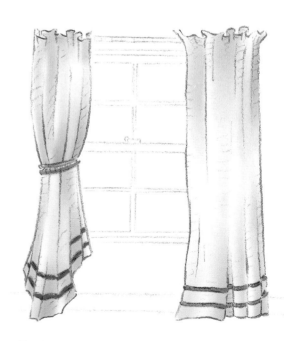

▲ Design simple curtains for the squatter sash windows often found in cottages.

◄A contemporary, informal curtain for a sash window.

►A low drape in sheer fabric allows light to filter through, leaving the window proportions visibly intact.

▲Long ties leave part of the window and the sky visible at all times; lightweight curtains pull across for privacy only.

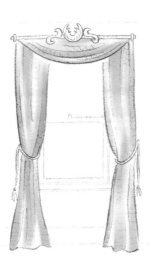

◄The most formal window and top treatments can be used for sash windows.

◄An informal, soft version of swag and tails dresses a simple side window to match a more formal bay window in the same room.

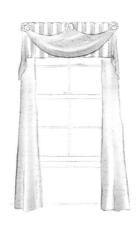

▲Simple curtains follow the scale of the window, while formal swags are held in place with traditional, painted rosettes.

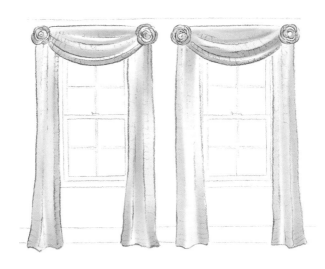

▲Curtains gathered over a pole in front of a recessed sash are held to the sides theatrically.

▲Double sash windows often occur in formal houses, a formal style of swags is relaxed with oversized fabric roses at the corners.

French Doors

Outward opening doors, whether single, double or multiple, may be curtained the same as any other window. Usually opening onto a garden or patio, curtains should be able to stack right back to the side. Tiebacks are usually needed to protect the curtains from gusts of wind and people walking in and out.
Inward opening doors can be a problem to curtain if there is little or no space at the sides. Fit an angled pole or track across the door wall and back onto the wall against the hinged side. Or fit a single curtain to a hinged rod which will swing back separately or with the door.

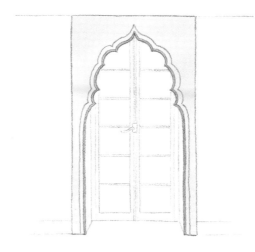

◄ Design a lambrequin to make a feature, a roller shade can be fitted at the top to pull down to the floor.

◄ If the outlook is particularly spectacular, drape fabric extravagantly to draw attention to the view in the manner of a good picture frame.

◄ Multiple doors should to be treated the same as the other windows in the room.

16

◄ Eyelet headings slotted over a pole pull back neatly into a corner or onto a side wall.

► Flat panels on crane rods swing into the recess, clear of the doors.

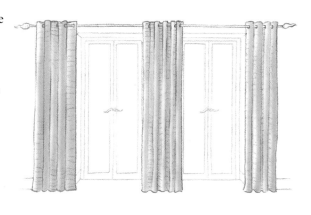

◄ Drape for effect only —for outward opening doors, the top can be draped lower than for those opening inwards.

► Flat curtains threaded onto fine poles stack back neatly. Fabric in similar tone to the walls will keep the view outside the focal point.

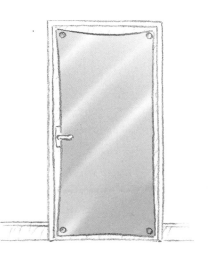

◄ Fit a heavy curtain as a certain cure for drafts from ill-fitting doors.

► Plain panels fixed to each corner cover the glass at night and lift off easily when not needed.

Skylights and Other Pivot Windows

Pivots: It is impossible to provide total privacy and allow open pivot windows at the same time. If you do need to cover and open at the same time, the best option is to fit some sort of shade or flat panel to the opening frame, angling the window to provide complete or partial privacy. Otherwise, curtains or shades can be fitted in front of the opening as long as they can be moved out of the way as the window pivots. Poles, tracks, valances and drapes are all possible, the design limited only by the situation and recess depth.

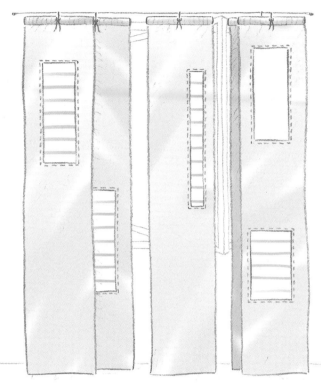

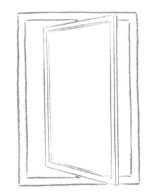

▲ Free-hanging panels can be arranged to cover almost the whole window. And if sheer, may be left across to filter and direct the light.

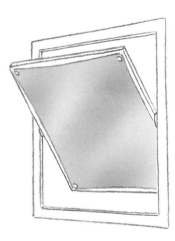

▲ Pinned panels can be removed for the day, or, if in a sheer fabric, left in place. The fittings need to be easy to operate, to allow for cleaning.

▲ An extravagant pole takes the attention away from a potentially ugly window by creating a more important line and shape. Plain curtains pull quietly out of the way allowing the pole to remain the center of attraction and the window to be purely functional.

▲ If there is space around the window, a traditional treatment is always possible. Where a pivot window is fitted in a room or area with other traditional shapes, they should all be treated the same. The only restriction is that any curtains should pull right back from the edges of the window.

Skylights: Privacy is seldom necessary but light might need to be filtered or controlled. Roller shades can be bought for any standard windows. Specialty shade companies will make up blinds in your own fabrics, as well as pleated, louvred and Venetian styles. Inexpensive plain shades can easily be painted or decorated with fabric paints or stencils, especially for children's rooms. If you can reach, flat panels in light voile or printed cotton can be fixed to each corner.

If you do want curtains, fix to battens or poles at the top and bottom of the recess and fix fabric between. Where long, floor-length curtains are possible and desirable, rein in with tiebacks where the window meets the wall.

▲A fun shape cut from board and fixed in front of the window creates a feature. The hole size will be governed by the amount you need to be able to open the window. If the window does not need to open fully, there is more scope for different shapes.

▲Curtains soften the window, but are often then out of reach, making opening and closing difficult or impossible. So use a curtain for decoration and fit a neat shade to the inside frame of the window.

▲Where the skylight is fitted low into a roof, there are more possibilities. Long curtains need to cover the top fittings, let light in and clasp back to the wall/roof joint. A roller shade fitted to the frame will still be useful for blackout. Sheer under-curtains may be used to soften the window at night, looped back with the curtains, which remain as dressing. For a study, landing or den, a heavy tapestry or a kelim would make interesting curtaining.

Picture Windows

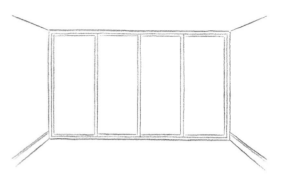

Some windows look best without curtains or shades, for example, picture windows with a panoramic view or windows which overlook a beautiful garden, which can be floodlit at night. However, for situations where some form of shades and curtains are needed, they should always be kept simple, so as not to detract from the view.

▲ Three layers of light curtaining provide for all eventualities. A deep cornice from the ceiling covers multiple tracking and the dead light above.

▲ Where there is heating below, shades cover the windows at night, sheer curtains filter light during the daytime.

▲ Use borders or complementary fabrics to pick up the strong horizontal line initiated by the pole.

▶ Wall-to-wall windows do not leave space for curtains to stack into. Flat panels remain over the window and slide across to filter light as needed.

◀ Not all picture windows reach the floor, but the curtains should.

▶ Functional curtains cover wall to wall, a draped top treatment covers the hardware and fills the dead light.

Dormer Windows

Dormer windows are set into sloping roofs and tend to be in attic rooms, although they can occur on the ground floor of an unusual building. They come in a variety of shapes and sizes and can be difficult to curtain without losing light. Curtains may be short, in a recess with a deep sill, or taller and to the floor.

The recess may be of equal depth all the way down or taper off towards the bottom of the window. Where the recess is deep enough, that is, as deep as half the width of the window, curtains can be fitted to crane rods, allowing the curtains to sit back against the side walls. Flat panels in firm or soft fabrics, quilted or bordered, will fall easily from a single crane or when clipped over hooks.

▲ Thick quilted panels are heavy enough to hold themselves straight even where the recess tapers to almost nothing.

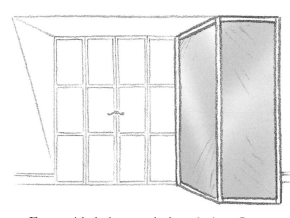

▲ A single, unlined curtain pulls right back to the side taking up little space.

▲ For a wide balcony window design, fix arms which will hold fabric under tension and swing back and fold like a screen.

▲ Roller shades take up little space, a fixed lambrequin hides unattractive sides and hardware.

▲ Long curtains outside the recess need to be simple and to draw back to allow enough light to enter.

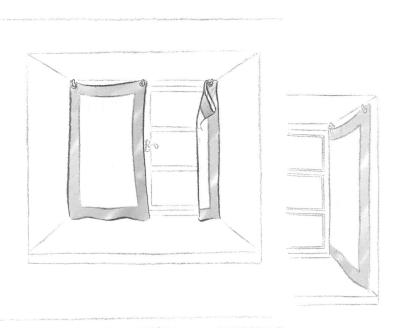

▲ Flat panels slip over hooks fixed to the window frame or against the sides of the recess.

▲ A thin wire holds a light curtain across the window, it can be looped up or folded back neatly to the side.

Arched Windows

Arched windows are always chosen for architectural value, as feature windows to direct attention to a pleasing outlook and to improve the building façade. In a period house or fine conservatory you may be blessed with a whole row but more usually they will be found as a single focal point: a clear light above a solid door or as the center of a Venetian window.
Arched windows don't need to be dressed. Curtaining is needed only to address the questions of privacy and light control.

▼Hang curtains with a fixed heading, then follow the window line to tie high for maximum light.

▼A flat panel on a crane rod will allow the door to open fully.

▼Heavy curtains may be needed for a cold area.
The deep headings balance the difficult "arch" gap.

▼Light curtains for privacy only
need to cover the main part of
the window.

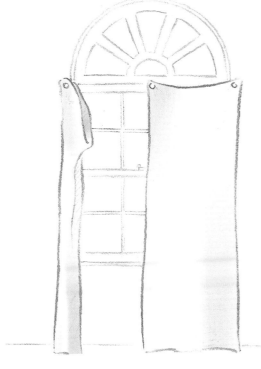

▼A decorative lambrequin dresses the spaces
around the window accentuating the arch itself.

▼A single curtain can be drawn back to show
off the whole window.

Double Windows

Usually double windows are proper pairs—well balanced and in good proportion. Curtaining can be as imaginative as you like, the two windows can be treated separately or as one unit. Uneven double windows are more difficult, but it can be challenging to design window treatments which will even up the visual aspect. Make use of shades, top treatments and side drapes to accommodate unevenness.

▲For a children's room, fixed lambrequin can be used to even up the sizes as well as being attractive and fun.

▲Double windows can be so close together that the best way is to treat them as a single window.

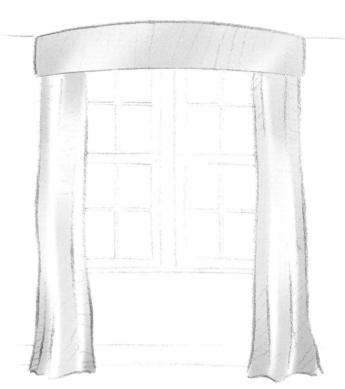

▲A curved cornice softens the squareness and balances the extra weight of double frames.

► Masses of fine fabric gathered over a curved bar make light, feminine curtaining for a bedroom or boudoir.

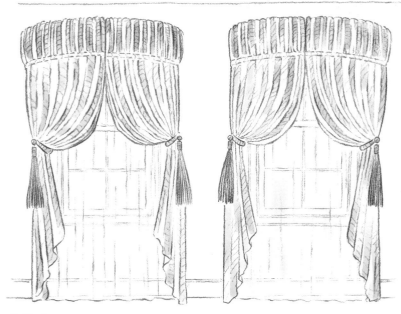

◄ Draped curtains dress both windows asymmetrically; shades pull down to cover the windows.

► Opposite sides are draped back and fixed; the curtains, sitting in the middle, draw across behind the drapes to cover the windows completely.

Casement Windows

In some countries casement windows open inward, in others outward. Where they open inward, curtains have to be able to be pulled right back to the sides, or the window will catch them as it is opened and closed.

Casement windows may also be doors, they may sit in deep recesses or flat on the wall, so there are as many ways to dress casements as there are curtains.

▲ Top treatments can be difficult with inward opening casements; here a simple draped swag catches the top of the window as it opens and closes.

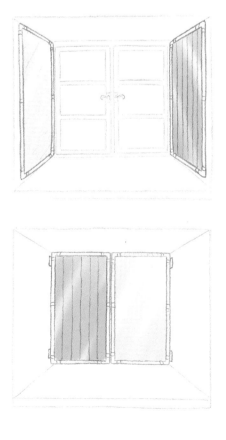

Metal frames fit onto the window frames and move either with the window or independently.

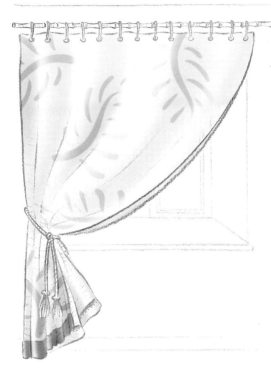

◄In a bathroom, a deep drape covers most of the window for privacy; a neat shade is fitted against the window at the back of the recess.

►Casement windows are not always the most attractive; sometimes the window treatment needs to be strong enough to detract from **the** window.

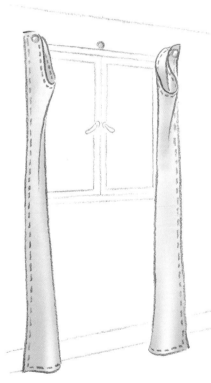

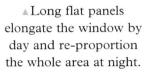

▲Long flat panels elongate the window by day and re-proportion the whole area at night.

▲Casement-opening windows or doors are used on many of the 20th century bay windows instead of the earlier sash windows. Most traditional and contemporary treatments will work.

CURTAIN DESIGNS

Blinds or Shades plus Curtains

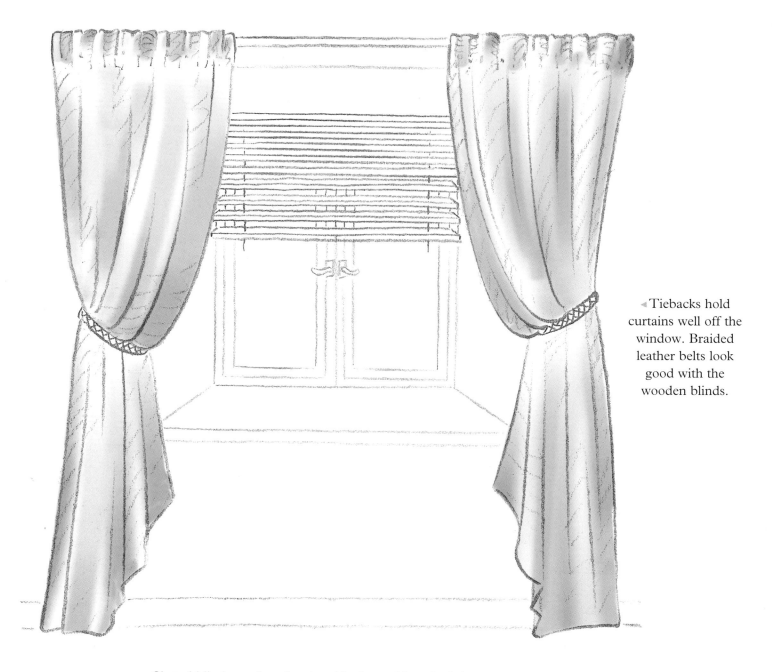

◄ Tiebacks hold curtains well off the window. Braided leather belts look good with the wooden blinds.

▲ Slatted blinds are functional and look good but don't keep out the cold. Heavy fabric gathered over a pole can be pulled across for colder evenings. For simplicity use a fabric which doesn't need lining or interlining—denim, wool blankets, antique hemp sheets, traditional bedcovers.

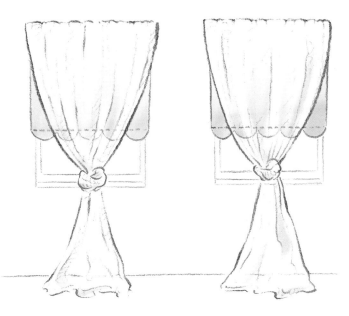

◄ Choose fabric for the shade which looks best flat and makes an interesting shape behind the sheer.

▲ Roller shades fit close to the window—leaving room for sheers to hang in front, in the same space. For double windows in particular, the architecture is softened but remains visible. A good way to cover double or rows of windows—also to even up odd 'pairs'.

▼ Light fabrics gather over wooden, metal or glass pole.

► Organdy, linen voile, organza, muslin, open weave linen, fine silks are all soft enough to filter but not cut out the light.

◄ Double tie a long sash to make a feminine tieback.

Rolled Shades

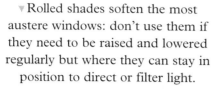

▼Rolled shades soften the most austere windows: don't use them if they need to be raised and lowered regularly but where they can stay in position to direct or filter light.

▲Use rolled shades to balance a too-wide or too-tall window.

▲Use up to three fabrics in one shade—top fabric, contrast lining and a third for the ties. Experiment with matte and shiny textures rather than pattern.

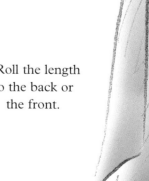

►Roll the length to the back or the front.

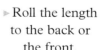

▼ Rows of shades need to hang at different levels
to keep the rolls apart.

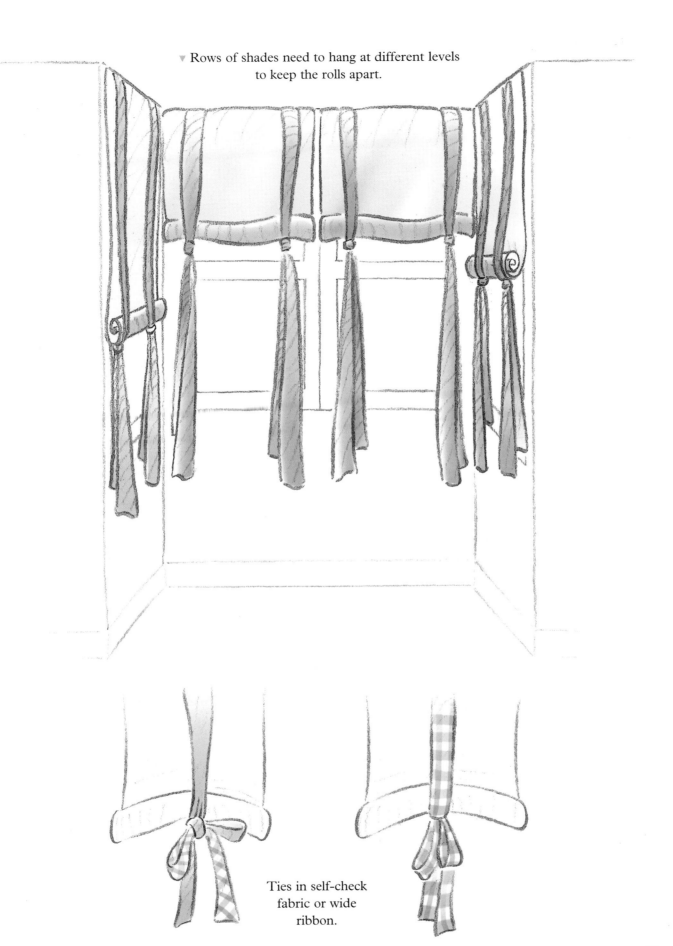

Ties in self-check
fabric or wide
ribbon.

Roman and Cascade Shades

▼Roman blinds—one solution to the classic short or long curtains dilemma.

▲Use borders or applied detail to make a statement when the shade is down and especially to bring a vertical line to a wide window.

▲Make curtains in same or complementary fabric.

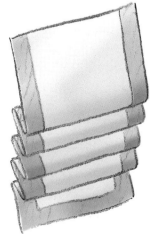

◄Plain fabric borders are smart: use tonal or textural contrast.

Decorative details

◄ **1:** Create a "border" with cord, rope, flat braid or leather thread.

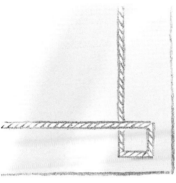

◄ **2:** Flat braid or grosgrain ribbon will bend to form interesting shapes.

◄ **3:** Choose decorative gimp or embroidered braid to complement the room style.

◄ **4:** Decorative stitching can also be employed to define and give weight.

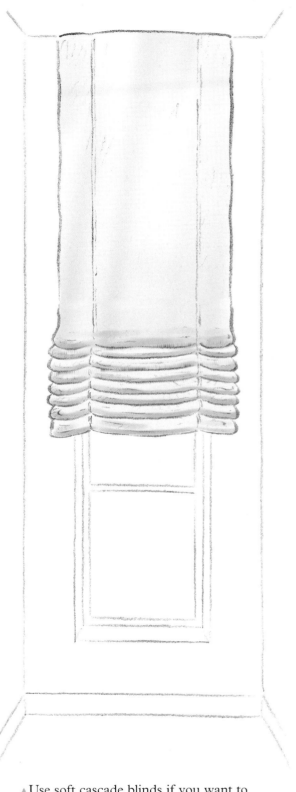

▲ Use soft cascade blinds if you want to reduce the strength of a stark window. Hang from the ceiling to balance a narrow tall window, to hide an ugly view or cover up disruptive hardware or pipes above.

Flat Panels: Bay Windows

Contemporary, economical, easy to make, easy to use and easy to clean, flat panels can be made to meet the demands of any and every style of window. Multiple tracks or poles facilitate interesting fabric combinations.

▼Flat panels are the answer for bay windows which can be difficult to curtain where there are shutters which pull out into the bay.

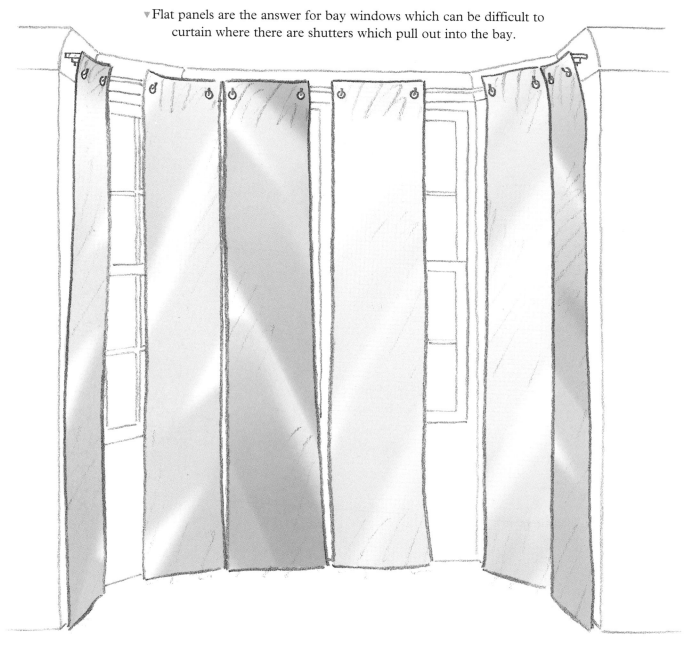

▲**Fabric choices 1:** Faux suede, brocades, wool panels, even strips of antique floor rugs should be long enough to brush the floor.

▲**2:** Sheer fabric panels cover the window permanently to obscure an ugly outlook or to maintain privacy.

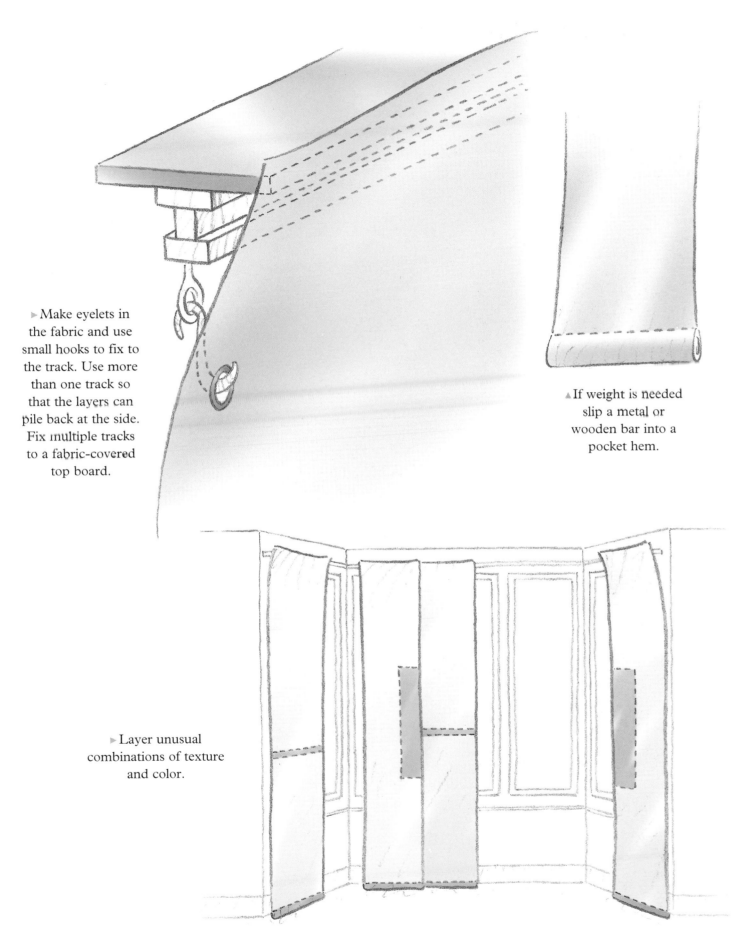

▶ Make eyelets in
the fabric and use
small hooks to fix to
the track. Use more
than one track so
that the layers can
pile back at the side.
Fix multiple tracks
to a fabric-covered
top board.

▲ If weight is needed
slip a metal or
wooden bar into a
pocket hem.

▶ Layer unusual
combinations of texture
and color.

Flat Panels: Minimalist Windows

▲ Curtains and minimalist windows just don't go. But if you need something, flat panels which swing across as needed are the best solution I can find. Choose fabrics with great care—interesting enough to make a point, stiff enough to hang elegantly, yet simple enough to be inconspicuous when not in use. Luckily there are very talented young designers producing incredible textiles using anything from metal threads to banana leaves. Seek them out.

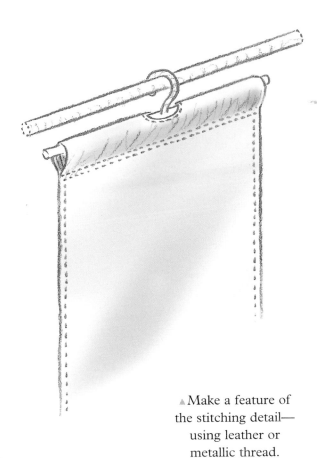

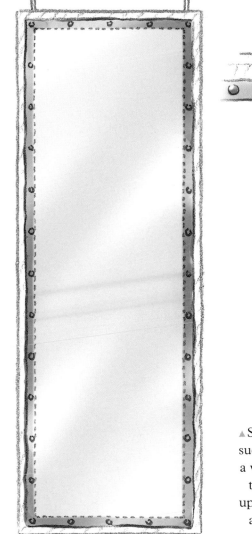

▲Make a feature of the stitching detail—using leather or metallic thread.

▲Go for the interesting texture— open weave linen scrim, metal threads through wool, blocks of high shine set into matte squares.

▲Solid wooden or metal frames commissioned from a joiner or smith make more solid window coverings. The double fitting can swing around a bay window. Any weight of fabric can be tacked to the wooden frame—use nails, drawing pins, tacks or studs.

▲Stretch faux or real suede or leather over a wooden frame and tack in place with upholstery nails. Use a separate tape to cover the raw edges if necessary.

Flat Panels: Picture Windows

▼Four different prints remain harmonious if chosen in a single colorway.

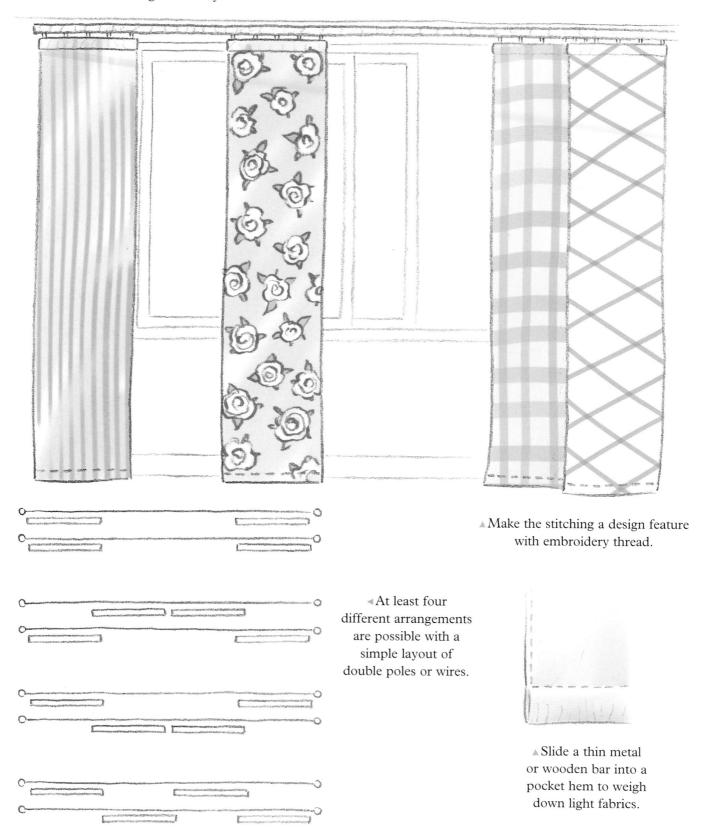

▲Make the stitching a design feature with embroidery thread.

◀At least four different arrangements are possible with a simple layout of double poles or wires.

▲Slide a thin metal or wooden bar into a pocket hem to weigh down light fabrics.

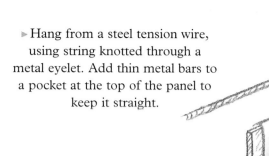

▶ Hang from a steel tension wire, using string knotted through a metal eyelet. Add thin metal bars to a pocket at the top of the panel to keep it straight.

▼ Position semi-sheer inset panels so that single layers offer tantalizing vignettes of the view outside.

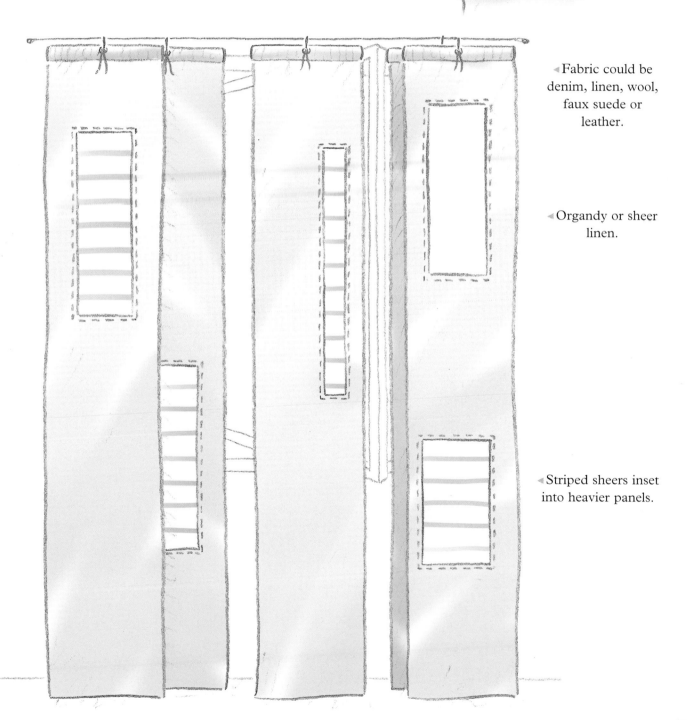

◀ Fabric could be denim, linen, wool, faux suede or leather.

◀ Organdy or sheer linen.

◀ Striped sheers inset into heavier panels.

Flat Panels: Conservatories

▲ Use fabric to create a picture at each window, e.g. a traditional toile de Jouy telling a story of everyday life.

▶ Handmade buttonholes loop over a simple hook to draw the panels back in neat folds.

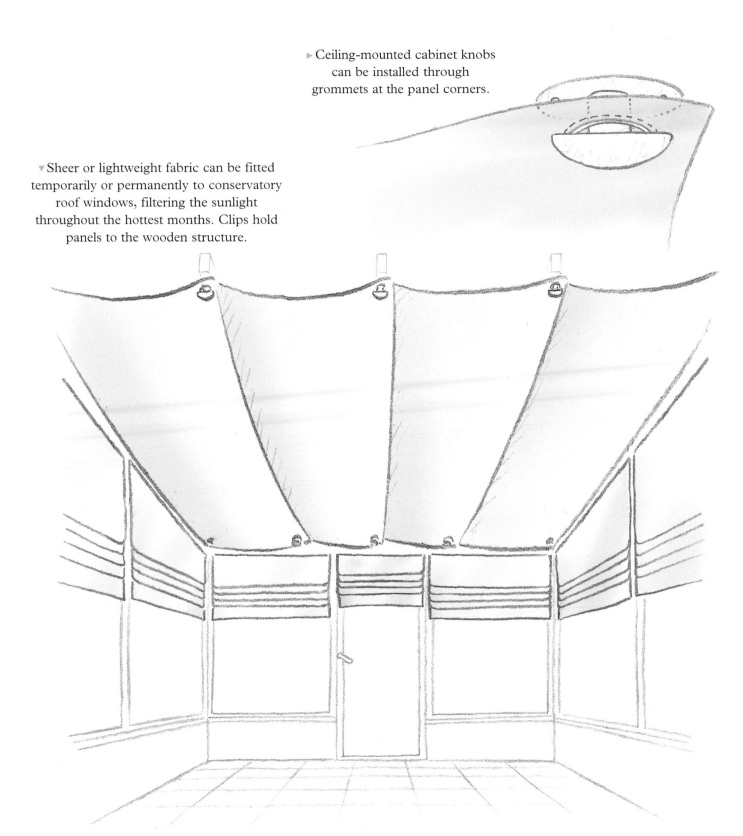

► Ceiling-mounted cabinet knobs can be installed through grommets at the panel corners.

▼ Sheer or lightweight fabric can be fitted temporarily or permanently to conservatory roof windows, filtering the sunlight throughout the hottest months. Clips hold panels to the wooden structure.

▲ Flat panels combine with soft Roman shades to cover odd windows, sloping sides and the roof of a simple garden room or conservatory. Keep the fabric simple and the same for each elevation.

Flat Panels: Casement Windows and Doors

◀ Soft panels take up minimum space and allow maximum light to enter.

▼ Where the recess is deep enough, hook curtains back against the side walls.

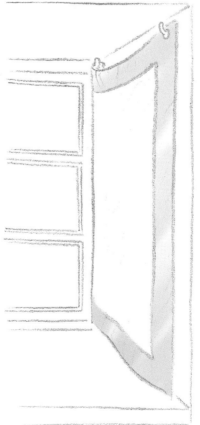

▼ Change the look for day and night—select two interesting patterns—one for each side. Play with borders, stripes, florals and checks.

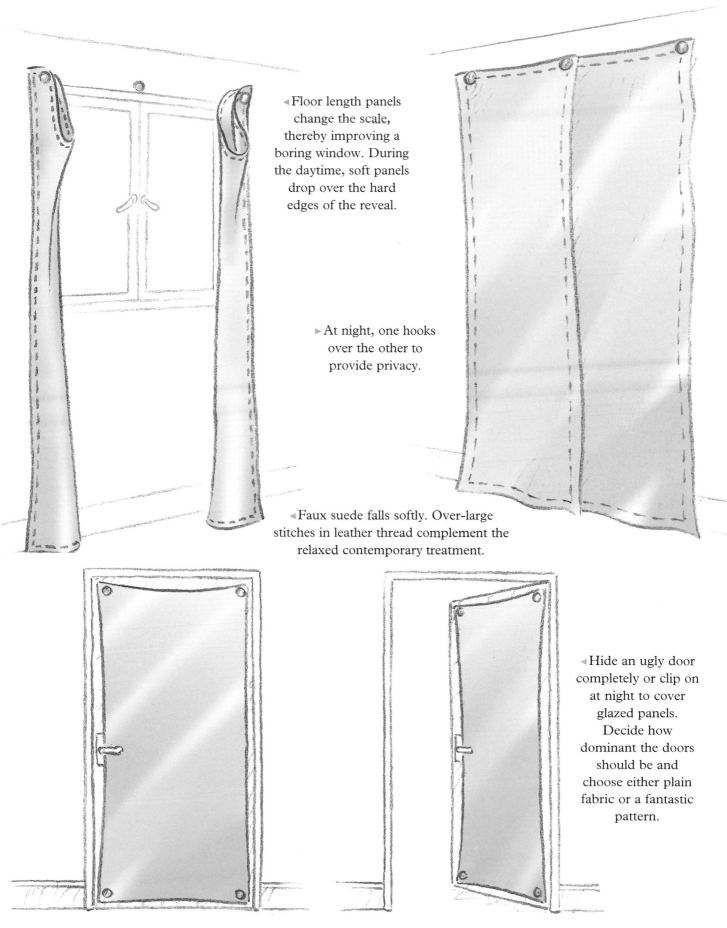

◄ Floor length panels change the scale, thereby improving a boring window. During the daytime, soft panels drop over the hard edges of the reveal.

► At night, one hooks over the other to provide privacy.

◄ Faux suede falls softly. Over-large stitches in leather thread complement the relaxed contemporary treatment.

◄ Hide an ugly door completely or clip on at night to cover glazed panels. Decide how dominant the doors should be and choose either plain fabric or a fantastic pattern.

Flat Panels: Square Bay and Recessed Windows

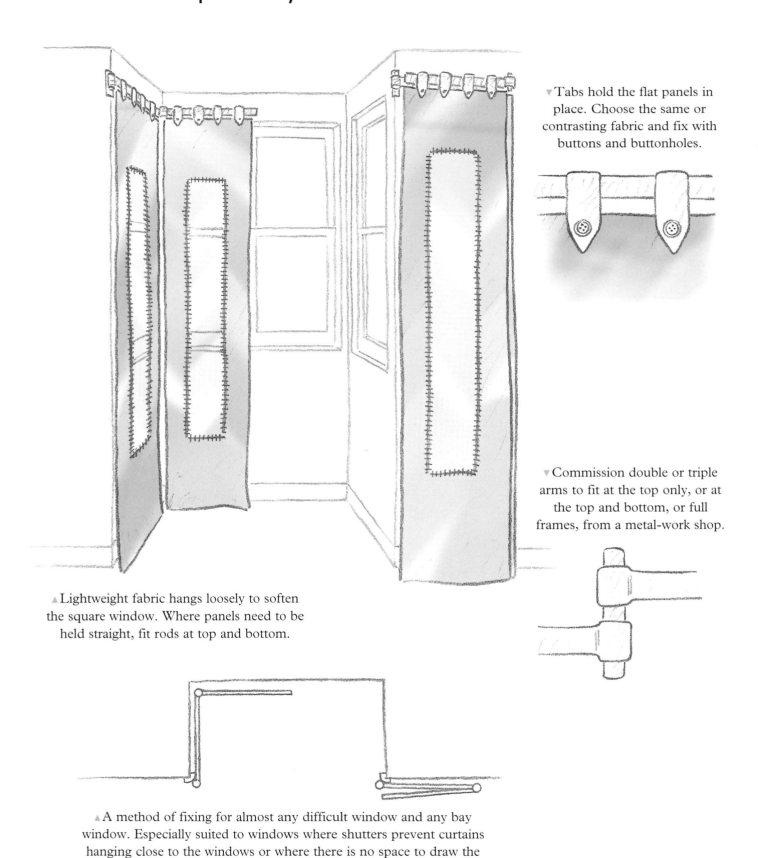

▼Tabs hold the flat panels in place. Choose the same or contrasting fabric and fix with buttons and buttonholes.

▼Commission double or triple arms to fit at the top only, or at the top and bottom, or full frames, from a metal-work shop.

▲Lightweight fabric hangs loosely to soften the square window. Where panels need to be held straight, fit rods at top and bottom.

▲A method of fixing for almost any difficult window and any bay window. Especially suited to windows where shutters prevent curtains hanging close to the windows or where there is no space to draw the curtains right away from the windows.

▼ Leather tabs fit around the bars of a full frame with jacket or tent studs.

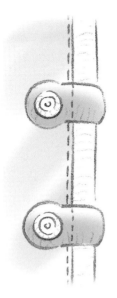

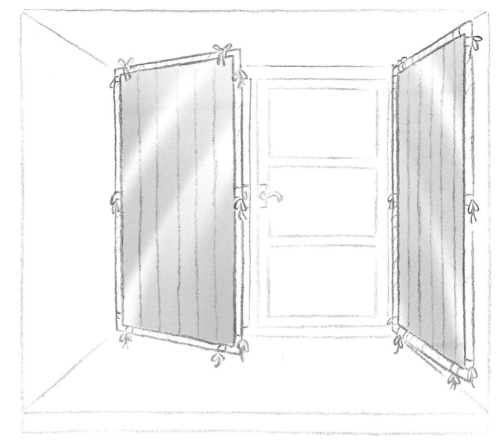

▲ Fabric panels fitted to a full frame open back against the sides of a deep recess.

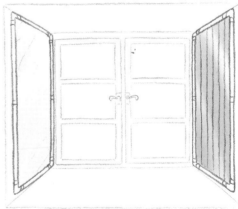

▶ Double-sided panels can be switched around if the top fabrics and lining have been chosen to work together.

▲ Tie panel in place onto a full frame using fabric, ribbon, cord, leather thonging or shoelaces.

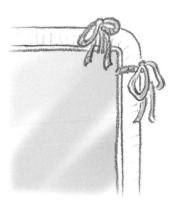

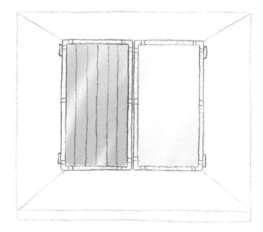

▶ Select contrast of texture, line or pattern. Perhaps a plaid with faux suede, stripe with plain, small check with large pattern.

Flat Panels: Recessed Casement Windows

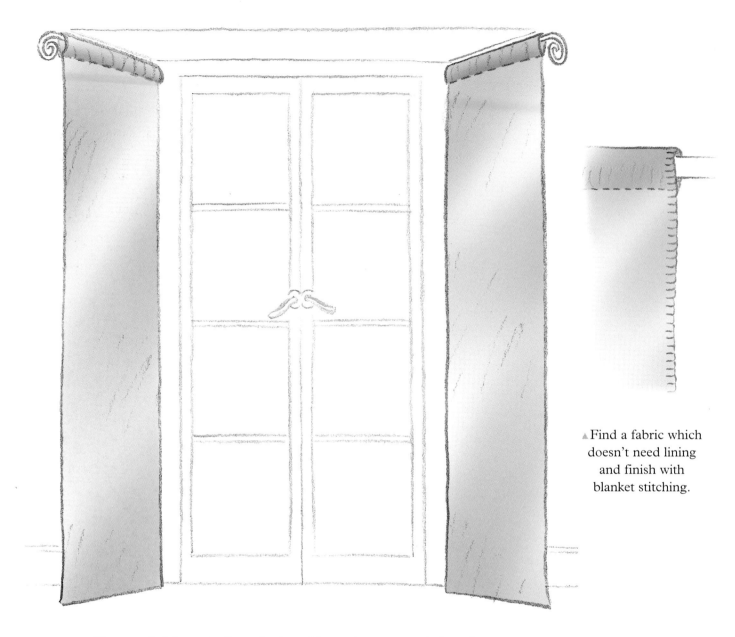

▲ Find a fabric which
doesn't need lining
and finish with
blanket stitching.

▲ Flat panelled "curtains" are the best thing to happen to windows in a
long time. I do hope their versatility ensure their place way beyond fashion.
They are absolutely perfect to fold back against a recess, so keeping the
window simple and maximizing the light potential at the same time.

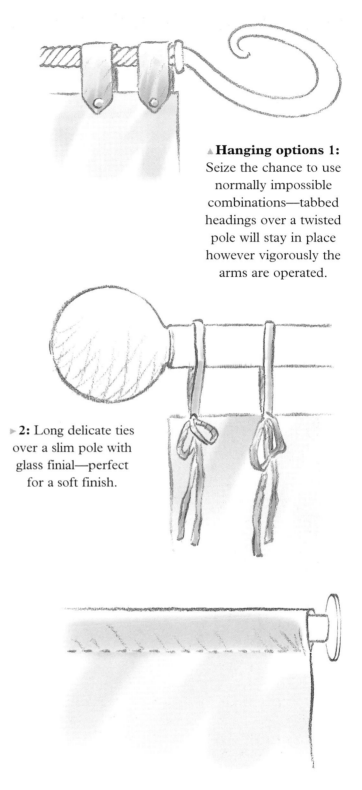

▲Both sides are equally important, so have fun with the fabrics. So little fabric is needed that for once you can choose something really expensive without breaking the budget!

▲**Hanging options 1:** Seize the chance to use normally impossible combinations—tabbed headings over a twisted pole will stay in place however vigorously the arms are operated.

▶**2:** Long delicate ties over a slim pole with glass finial—perfect for a soft finish.

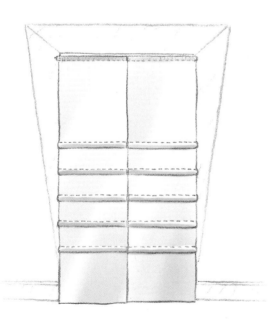

▲Pleat one fabric or choose several colors joined with open flaps to make strong, definite horizontal lines.

▲**3:** A simple bar holds the fabric flat—you will need some sort of end to stop the panel falling off.

Flat Panels: Doors

▶ Double crane rods holding different fabrics close over each other, combining a practical solution with decorative furnishing. A brilliant solution to liven up an awkward space: a boring corridor or the sort of deep recess that can result from an unsympathetic building extension or conversion.

▶ Use panels on crane rods to cover front doors, both for a neat look and where there is no room for curtaining to stack back. This is a good solution for all doors with glazed panels.

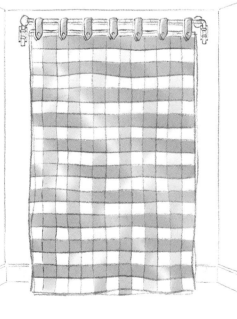

◀ An inspired combination of semi-sheer layers—one with horizontal and the other with vertical stripes, layer to make squares.

▶ Fabric panels sit flat back against the wall.

Antique textile table covers, tapestries, floor rugs or commissioned painted or worked lengths make decorative hangings by day and practical coverings at night. Use heavy fabrics to combat drafts completely or light fabrics for softness and interesting combinations.

Eyelet Headings

▼Eyelets fitted into the top of the curtain are threaded over a pole of lesser diameter. Stylish in a contemporary situation, the fabric folds back neatly to one or both sides of the window or door. So this is also a good solution for where the stack-back space is limited. The curtain panels may be almost flat when pulled across or as full as you wish. Choose fabrics which express the overall design style. Any fabric which doesn't need to be lined can be used—tapestries, leather, suede, denim, wool, linen and cotton.

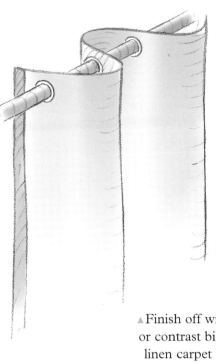

◄Poles may be wood, metal or fine twisted tension wire.

▲Finish off with a self or contrast binding— linen carpet tape or wide flat braids—or strips of the same fabric wrapped around the raw edges.

▲A good solution for a contemporary bay window, especially where there is little stack-back. You'll need to order a wooden or metal pole from an installer who can bend to fit your measurements. Choose whether you want two or four curtains and make sure, if you prefer two, that the pole will be strong enough with just one center fixing.

▲Where there is little space to the hinge side of the door, bend the pole around onto the side wall. If there are pipes or boxing in the corner, just have the pole bent around them.

Tab Headings

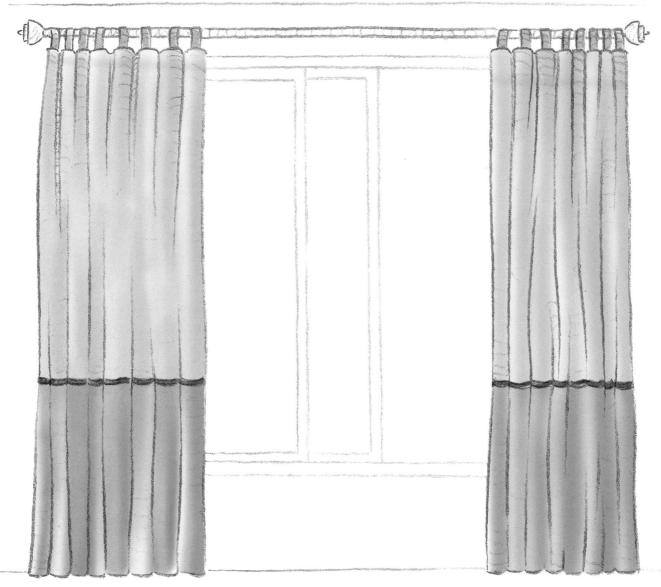

Tab headings are neat and simple. The only restriction is that unless you buy special flat rings that sit under each tab, you can only draw the curtains if you can reach to ease the tabs along by hand. If the window or door opens inwards the curtains will need to pull, otherwise just hook the curtains back to the sides.

▲ For a neat look, the curtains should just skim the floor. Two fabrics joined by a decorative strip of fabric or braid make a simple situation more interesting.

Tab designs 1: Faux suede or leather strips with heavy stitching detail.

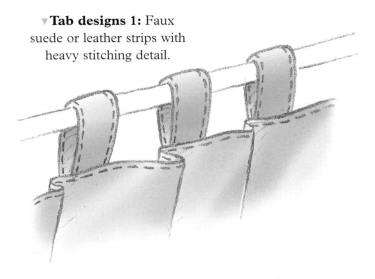

2: Long thin tabs lighten the whole effect—use for a shower curtain and to relieve dead light.

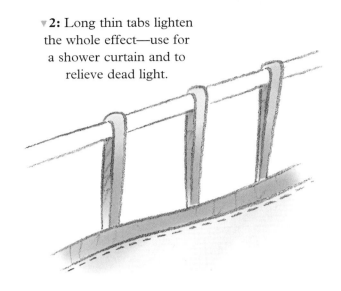

3: Separate tabs close over the curtain with double-sided studs.

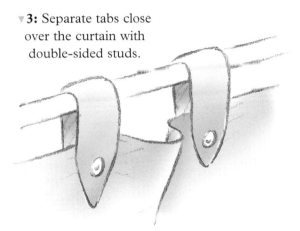

4: Stitch tabs into the curtain, using alternate colors of a striped fabric.

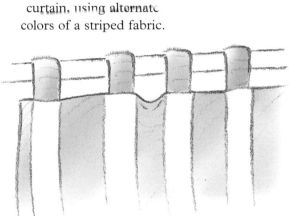

5: Find suitable or unusual buttons and make hand-sewn buttonholes in shaped tabs.

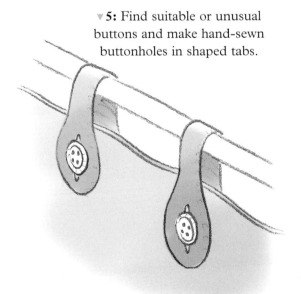

6: A no-sew solution, metal studs from camping suppliers look good and can be quick to fit.

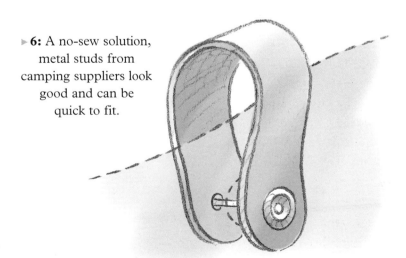

Tie Headings

Ties are the most feminine headings, satisfying for girlie bedrooms, boudoirs and dressing rooms. Some chunkier ties may be used sparingly and with great care for more formal windows.

▲ A glass dragonfly brooch looks great pinned to this light, flowing silk.

▲ Radiators can be a problem with long curtains—shades are good as the first line of defense against the night and drafts. This soft shade complements the informal curtains—ties could be checked, plain, of ribbons, fabric or tape. Use the shade on its own, or pull the curtains over as well, leaving the sides pinned back.

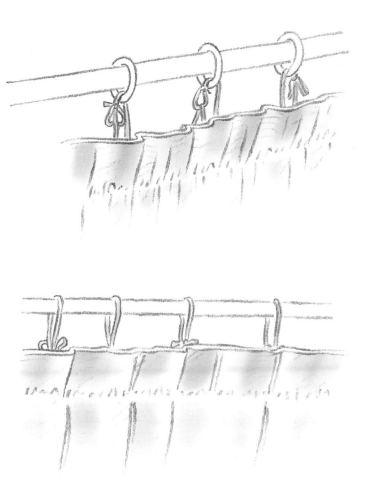

◄ Tie details 1:
Ties on wooden or metal rings
pull easily and look pretty.

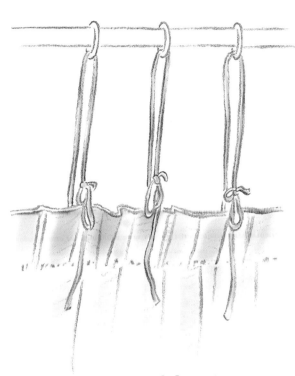

▲ 3: Ties straight on the
pole are fine if the
headings are fixed or
you can reach the pole
to ease them along.

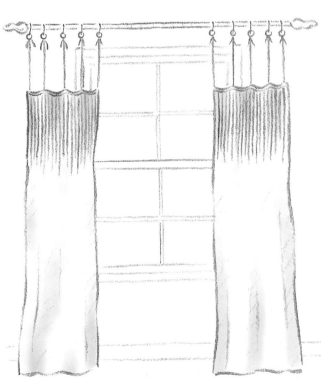

▲ 2: Long ties look good if
the curtains don't need to
come to the top of a
window or if the dead light
is very deep, e.g. picture
windows, shower curtains,
long tall windows.

◄ 4: Long ties, glass pole,
pin tucks, lightweight linen,
gathered headings—all
delicate elements to keep
the curtains light and fun.

Fixed Headings

Fixed headings are only suitable for windows which are taller than they are wide, with curtains falling to or onto the floor. If you are unsure, pin a sheet over one half of your window, drape it back and see how the hemline falls. Then use string and safety pins to hold the "curtain" back in several different places to find your preferred hook back position.

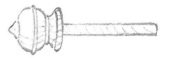

▲Wood, glass or metal shapes should be on stems long enough for the whole curtain to loop over.

▲Quite a decorative treatment for this simple window, but the high hook back and curtain draping back from the recess allows maximum light to enter the room.

▲Although primarily decorative, fixed headings can provide good solutions to some problems. A simple window at the end of a long corridor can be transformed into a feature. Curtaining over a tall, thin window may be used to direct the light low into the room. Ugliness above, in or outside the window can be concealed behind the draped tops. Remember that fabric, especially silks, draped over glass will suffer from the effects of sunlight. Choose between linings or early replacement.

▲Extravagant bows from ribbons or fabric create theatrical effect.

▲Linings become as important as the main fabric especially where the drapes start higher. Use the opportunity for contrast of texture, pattern or color. Country block checks work effectively in a rural home and sophisticated line checks for an elegant window.

◀Rows of crystal droplets threaded onto silky threads plaited around the curtain sparkle in both day and artificial light.

Fixed Headings: Curved

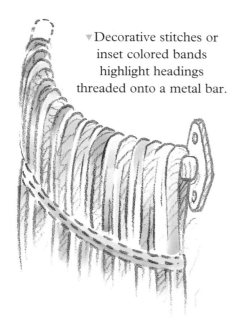

▼Decorative stitches or inset colored bands highlight headings threaded onto a metal bar.

▶Glass drops and long silk tassels are exquisite decoration for simple, elegant curtains.

▲Double windows need delicate handling if the curtaining is not to overpower. Light fabrics in classical shape allow the windows to speak for themselves. Sheer under-curtains help to protect the fabric from sunlight.

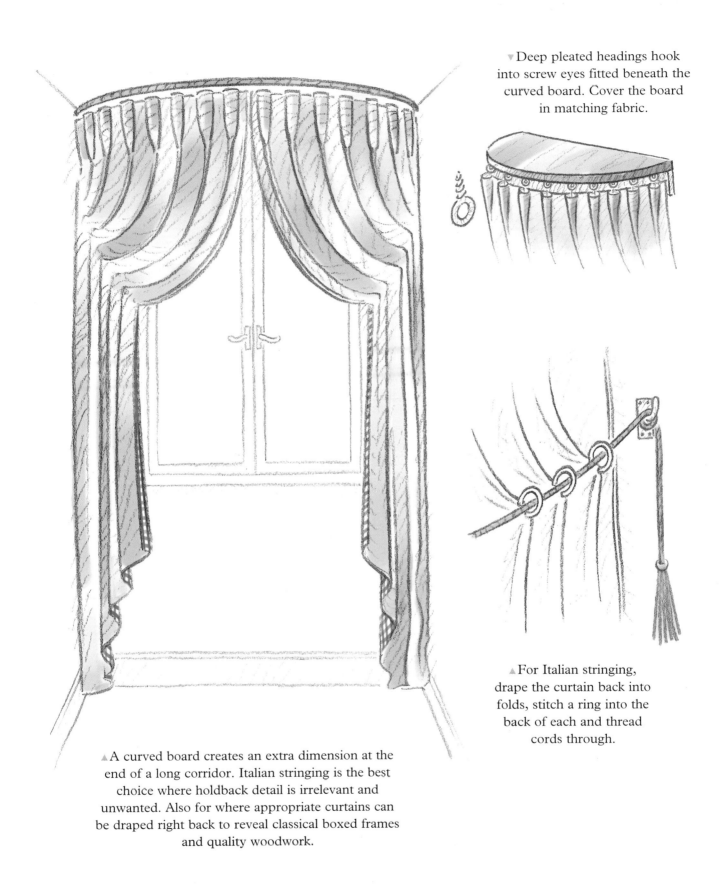

▼Deep pleated headings hook into screw eyes fitted beneath the curved board. Cover the board in matching fabric.

▲For Italian stringing, drape the curtain back into folds, stitch a ring into the back of each and thread cords through.

▲A curved board creates an extra dimension at the end of a long corridor. Italian stringing is the best choice where holdback detail is irrelevant and unwanted. Also for where appropriate curtains can be draped right back to reveal classical boxed frames and quality woodwork.

Fixed Headings Gallery

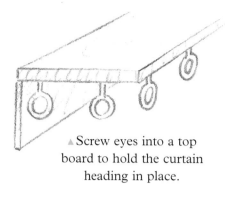

▲ Screw eyes into a top board to hold the curtain heading in place.

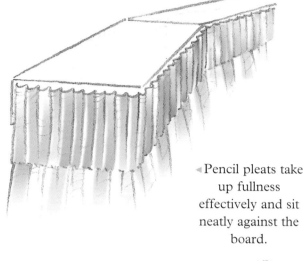

◄ Pencil pleats take up fullness effectively and sit neatly against the board.

▼ Make headings anything from 1½" to 8" (3.8 to 20.5 cm) deep to balance the window height.

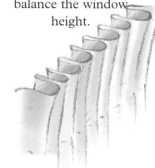

◄ A corsage of roses makes a pretty holdback for a bedroom.

◄ If you never need to draw back the curtains, join the headings together at the top and tie back as high as possible to maximize the available light. Fit blinds behind to use with or instead of the curtains.

◄ Overlong curtains drape on the floor to complement the pretty holdbacks.

Curtains don't always need to pull away from the window—consider imaginative combinations of ties, loops, tabs, buttonholes, hooks, bars and arms, as appropriate.

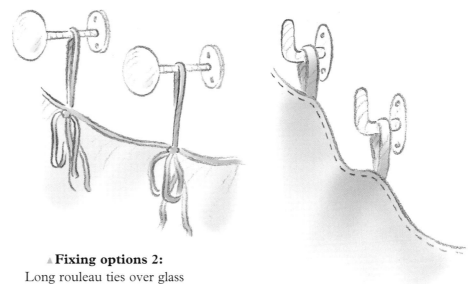

▼Fixing options 1:
Tabs over fixed hooks allow the curtain to be removed easily for regular cleaning—say in front of a shower, or over a kitchen window or door.

▲Fixing options 2:
Long rouleau ties over glass and metal holdbacks.

▲Fixing options 3:
Use any cup-shaped hooks—check out the antiques market for interesting ideas.

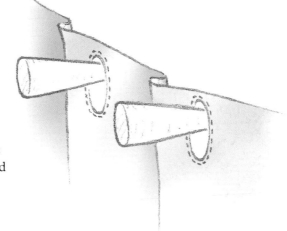

▶Fixing options 4:
Shiny metal pegs hold faux suede.

▲Keep curtains short for a neat look or overlong to soften.

▼Fixing options 5:
Wide loops slip easily over old rustic hat and coat hooks.

Pleated Headings and Hems

For more formal curtains the fullness is best taken up into pleated headings: usually between 2¾" and 9¾"(7 and 25 cm) deep to balance window height and fit with the overall design style.

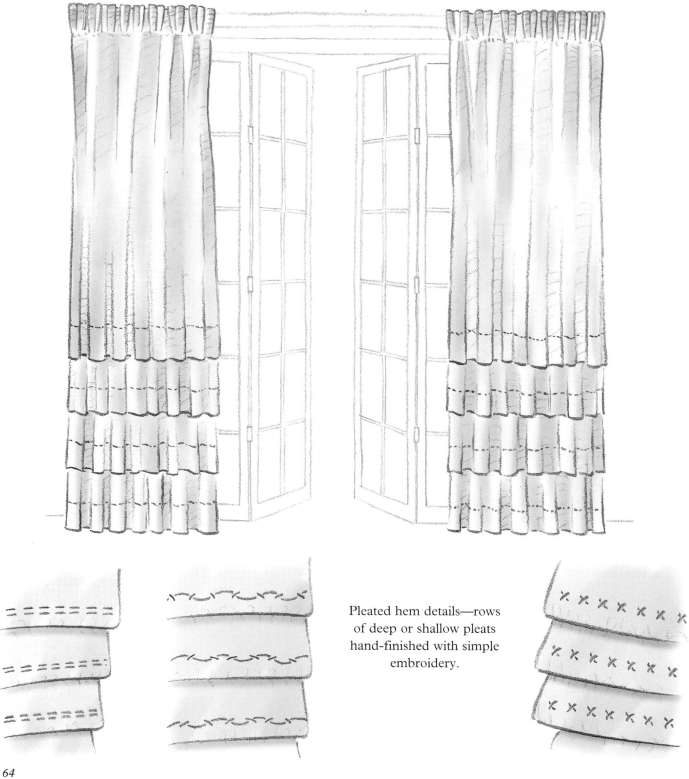

Pleated hem details—rows of deep or shallow pleats hand-finished with simple embroidery.

▽ **Pleating options 1:**
Double pleats left open at the top, stitched together at the bottom.

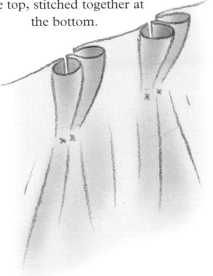

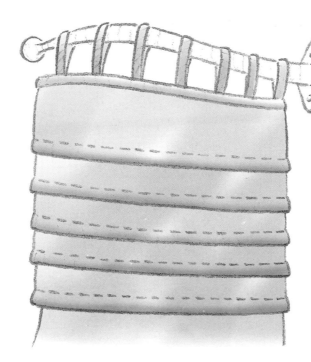

◁ **2:** Rows of pleats add interest to the top of a flat panel with tabbed heading.

▽ **3:** Stitch pleats together at the top and leave the bottom open so that the fabric hangs straight. You might need to stuff the pleat at the top to hold the shape.

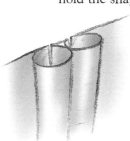

▷ **5:** Pull together at the bottom for a goblet-shaped pleat.

▽ **4:** Triple pleats for the fullest curtains—always stitch together at the bottom and usually leave open at the top.

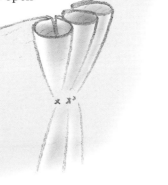

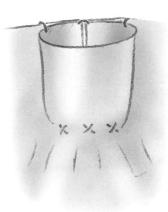

▷ **6:** Secure the top edges and along the bottom to make a flat/boxed pleat.

Rod-pocket Headings

▲ The pocket needs to be very much wider than the pole if you want to pull the curtains back at all.

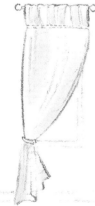

◄ Wherever a heading can be fixed, a rod pocket is an option–a prettier heading than tabs or panels.

► Fabric folded over to the front makes a self-valance which stays put when the curtains are tied back.

A flat piece of fabric attached to the curtain underneath the gathered heading creates a more formal valance.

Leave the fabric edge plain or finish with stitching, braid or contrast bindings.

Gather closely or make a frill above the pole.

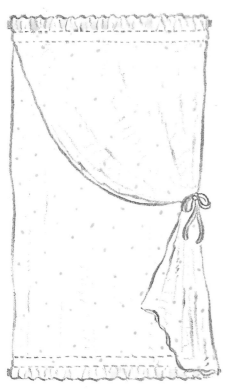

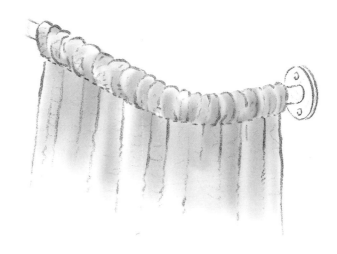

Two layers of curtaining are gathered together onto one pole at the top; the under layer is gathered onto another pole at the bottom, providing privacy. Tie the top layer to one side.

Good wherever you want to cover the pole completely.

Pleating Details

A simple, elegant window treatment using plain fabrics in complementary textures. The outer curtains without decoration, the sheers behind detailed with multiple rows of fine pleats.

▲ Use pleats to make a light fabric more dense, especially below a window where the see-through quality might be a disadvantage.

▲ Pleated hems usually provide their own weight; if needed, run chain weight inside the lowest pleat.

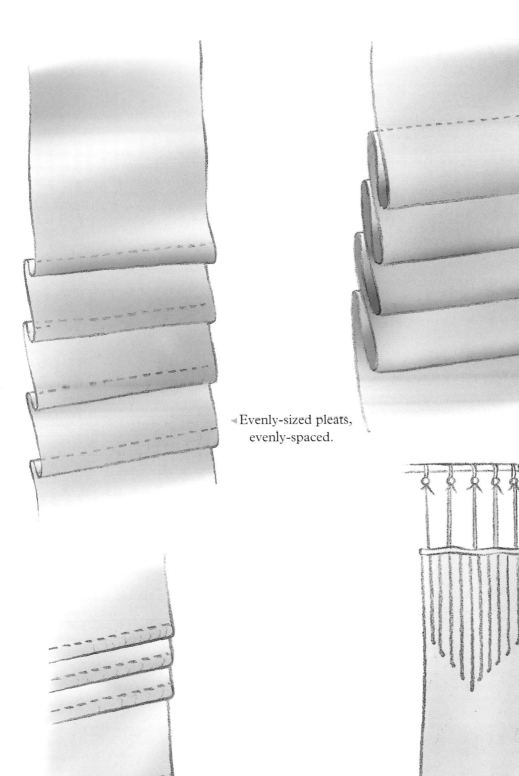

◄Overlapping pleats
may be even or varied,
becoming deeper
toward the hem.

◄Evenly-sized pleats,
evenly-spaced.

◄Fine pin tucks in
ordered, inverted-
triangle form.

◄Wide rows of two,
three and more pleats
spaced apart.

69

Lengthening or Shortening Existing Curtains

Curtains often last longer than any one house move. With imagination some curtains can be lengthened or shortened to fit a new location. If you move frequently or prefer in any case not to make curtains, then try blankets, bedcovers, sheets or tablecloths—any interesting fabric and color which may be hung, lengthened or shortened easily.

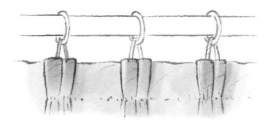

▲ Adjustment might be as simple as re-hooking so that a curtain whose heading previously covered the pole now hangs from below.

▲ Any curtain can be lengthened by adding a deep hem in complementary fabric. Choose a similar or heavier weight of fabric with similar fiber content. Emphasize the join with a braid or top stitch to make it a feature.

◄ To shorten, fold over the top and clip with decorative curtain clips.

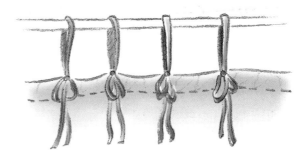

▲ Lengthen ties to make the curtain "longer".

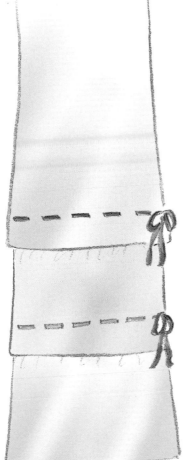

► Pleat a long length to shorten, make eyelets and thread string or ribbon through for decoration.

▼ **Added panels 1:** Add a new section to an existing curtain with string threaded between two rows of eyelets.

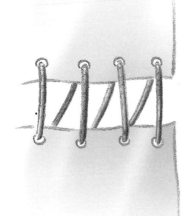

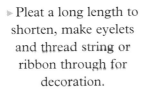

▲ **Added panels 2:** Use buttons and buttonholes to join complementary panels.

► **Added panels 3:** Join new panels with buttonholes and toggles.

Borders

As well as being simply decorative, borders provide a multitude of solutions to a whole range of window curtaining problems. Just a few examples—to lengthen curtains, to add width, to introduce another color or another texture, to bring out a particular color, to lighten or weight the curtain fabric. Or to make a fashion change—say from fringing to a flat braid.

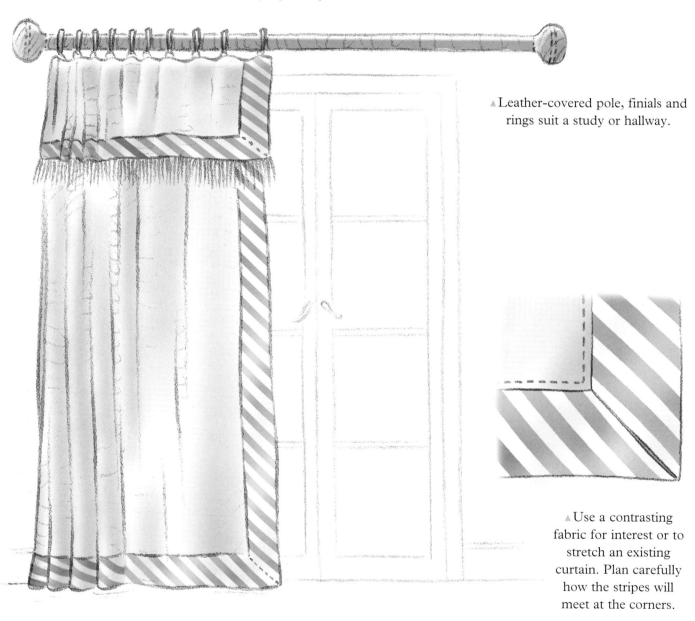

▲Leather-covered pole, finials and rings suit a study or hallway.

▲Use a contrasting fabric for interest or to stretch an existing curtain. Plan carefully how the stripes will meet at the corners.

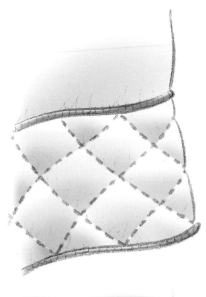

▶ Border details 1: A tonally-contrasted deep border relieves the busyness of a multi-paned window. Or it could be stitched in as a horizontal stripe just below sill height.

◀ 2: Add a quilted panel of the curtain fabric piped in a complementary tone.

◀ 3: Inset a contrast border with prominent topstitching across the seam.

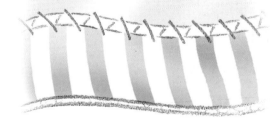

▶ 4: A plain inset panel relieves a striped fabric. Stitch to attach or use eyelets and lacing cord.

▼ 5: Add a plain fabric to a print or stripe. For integrity accentuate the join with topstitching, threaded with raised cord.

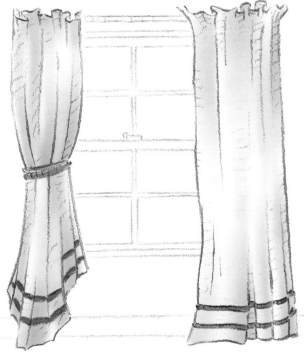

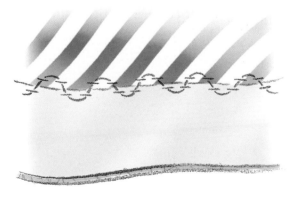

▲ 6: Double lines can be made with inset fabric or, more easily, with applied flat braid.

Edgings

The possibilities for interesting and exciting bordered edges are immense. Changes of texture, color and style are limited only to imagination and resources. In all cases there should be an element of tension—the marrying of masculine and feminine, the yin and yang, the expected with the unexpected. Fashion will play a real part in the type of fabrics and trimmings that are available.

As well as the classic combination of stripes and checks added to plain or pattern, try leather with flowers, lace with tartan plaid, suede with linen sheer, organdy with linen, silk with tweed, glass with wool. Just be careful that if the curtains need to be washed or cleaned regularly, both the main fabric and border are of the same fiber content and weight.

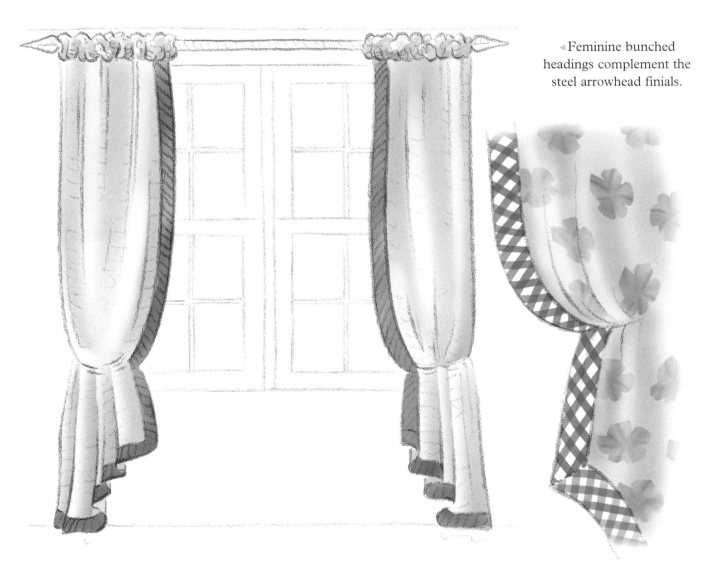

◀ Feminine bunched headings complement the steel arrowhead finials.

▲ Try a leather ribbon or book-binding edging, either plain or embossed, applied to wool, linen or any brocades and tapestry fabrics. Or use to weight a wool challis or linen sheer.

▲ On a typical country window, a small check provides the masculine to the feminine floral print.

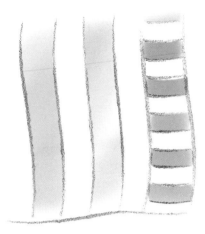

▲ Edging details 1:
Stay with the same color and design but change the scale.

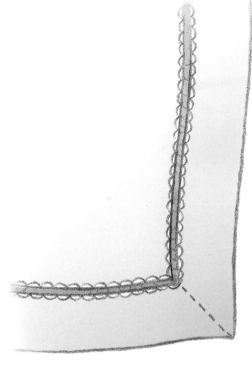

▲ 2: Mix textures as much as you like—here silk ribbon over cotton lace.

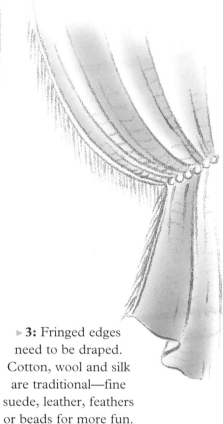

▶ 3: Fringed edges need to be draped. Cotton, wool and silk are traditional—fine suede, leather, feathers or beads for more fun.

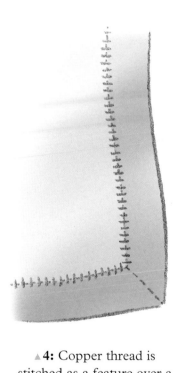

▲ 4: Copper thread is stitched as a feature over a faux suede border added to a country linen.

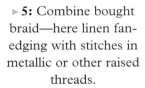

▶ 5: Combine bought braid—here linen fan-edging with stitches in metallic or other raised threads.

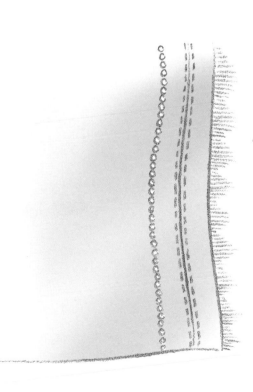

▲ 6: If you like to embroider, show off your faggoting. Use plain weaves—try organdy with linen.

Two Layers

Layers of curtains and shades offer interesting and challenging decoration possibilities as well as performing valuable function. Under-curtains or shades in sheer fabrics filter daylight in a workroom or protect furnishings. They might also be hiding a poor outlook or providing privacy. Shades can be lowered to leave a radiator free, with the heavier or top layers of curtains pulled across later in the day or not at all.
Use layers for fun, to alter the balance of your windows, to alter the perspective and outlook, to luxuriate in stunning fabrics, to provide effective solutions to the extremes of light and dark, heat and cold.

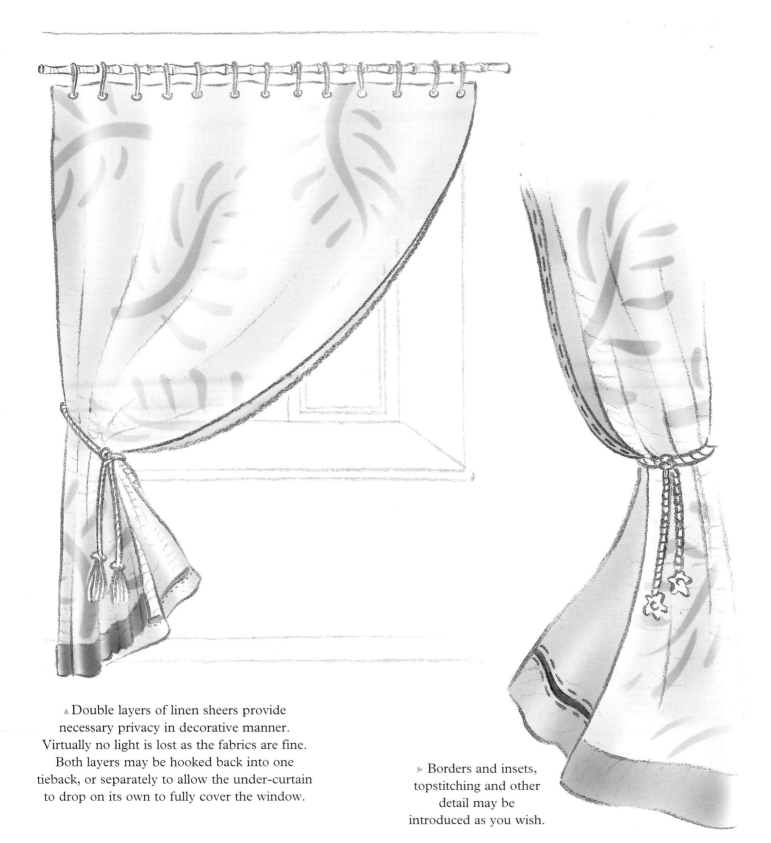

▲Double layers of linen sheers provide necessary privacy in decorative manner. Virtually no light is lost as the fabrics are fine. Both layers may be hooked back into one tieback, or separately to allow the under-curtain to drop on its own to fully cover the window.

▶ Borders and insets, topstitching and other detail may be introduced as you wish.

Three Layers: Double and Bay Windows

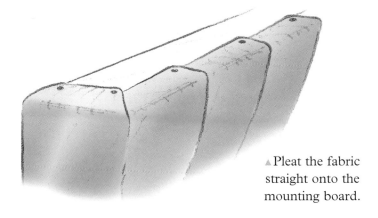

▲ Pleat the fabric straight onto the mounting board.

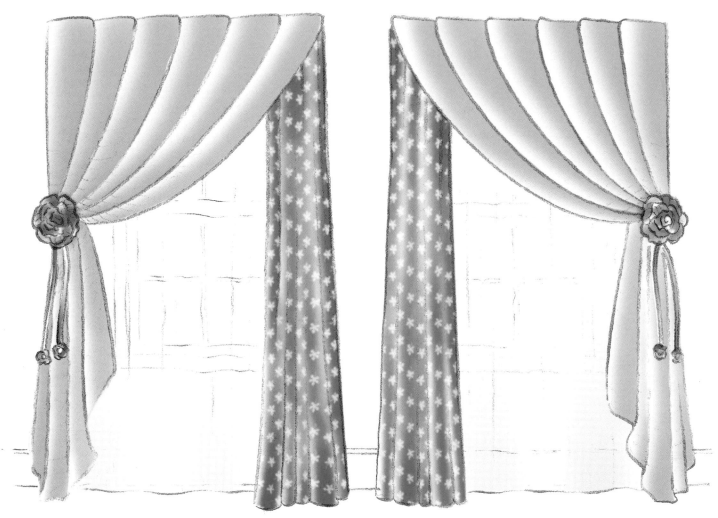

▲ Double windows need special consideration. These drapes could be extremely dramatic in rich colors and textures, heavy damasks, velvets, brocades and wools. Or absolutely understated in draped linens, soft silks or cottons. The symmetry of the curtaining is important, however the corsage holdbacks could be daringly different.

▲ The fixed curtain can be tied back much higher if you prefer—perhaps then with cords and tassels. Or dropped even lower to hide an ugly view—in which case use sheer fabric to allow the light to filter in.

▲Fixed curtains at the outer sides of the bay with a center swag provide elegance. Two pairs of under-curtains do the work: sheers at the back to filter sunlight with a fine brocade to pull across against the night. Choose good quality fabric in subtle colors to prevent the whole becoming over-theatrical. Unless, of course, that's just the effect you are after.

▲A long padded swath of fabric has been doubled around to hold the curtains in shape.

Three Layers with Cornice

Design layers of curtaining which help improve the balance of window to room. If curtains must go from wall to wall, or if the window really is too small for *the wall, this is a good way to retain some impression of height and to make a small window look bigger.*

▲Blanket stitching the edge of the under-curtain wittily complements the blanket style of the outer curtains.

▲Ties can be in string, jute, cotton, linen or wool with double or single tassels.

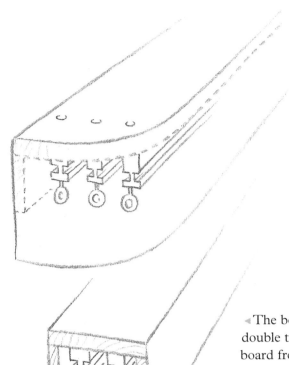

◄ Cornice boards in wood hold three rows of curtain tracks efficiently and provide a solid surface against which to fit fabric top treatments. Curve the board if you want to soften a square room.

◄ The board can be shallower for double tracking. Always cover the board front with the curtain fabric to hide the hardware.

▲ Picture windows provide the most wonderful views, but can be quite severe and extremely unfriendly when all is dark outside. Layers of soft fabrics pull right back in the daytime, overlapping to create good insulation at night. At least one layer in check or stripe will serve to echo the architectural quality of the window. Otherwise choose fabrics to complement the design style of the room.

Draped Curtains

▼Always elegant, draperies may be either carefully
cut or, for simple window dressings, just lengths of fabric
draped and pinned.

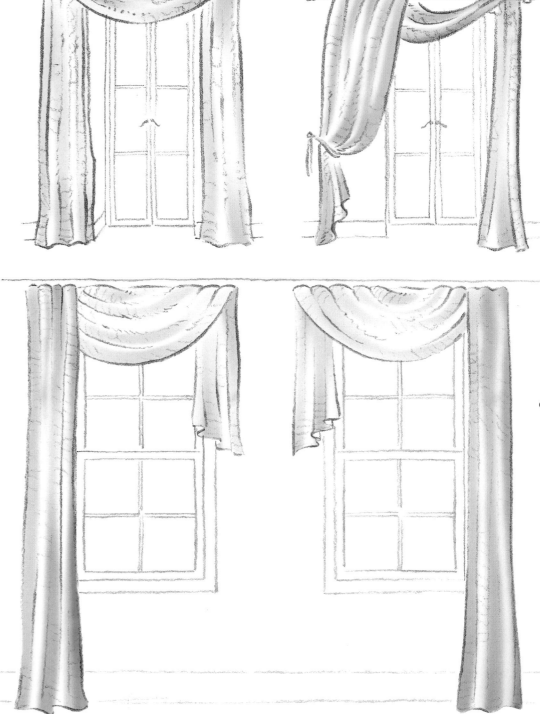

◄For decoration only,
cut a single piece for
each section and pin to
the top board.

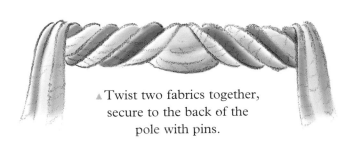

▲ Twist two fabrics together, secure to the back of the pole with pins.

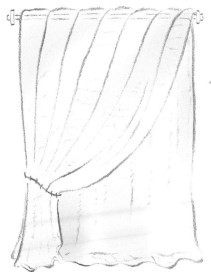

◀ Fold a long length over a fine pole. Drape the top layer back to one side, leaving the under layer down for privacy.

▲ Cut swag lengths on the cross for the smoothest drape.

◀ An exotic length of fabric is rolled over and over a fixed pole, caught back at the sides with twists of cord.

Draped Top Treatments

The soft drape over the top will catch onto the window—fine if you can reach the top and ease the fabric over, if not, hang the pole higher.

Inward opening casement—curtains need to be clear of the sides.

This rafia twist tieback is good for a seaside house.

Antique linen sheeting sits on the floor and pulls back casually—good for informal country house, holiday house, bathroom. Find silks or soft weaves for a taller, elegant window.

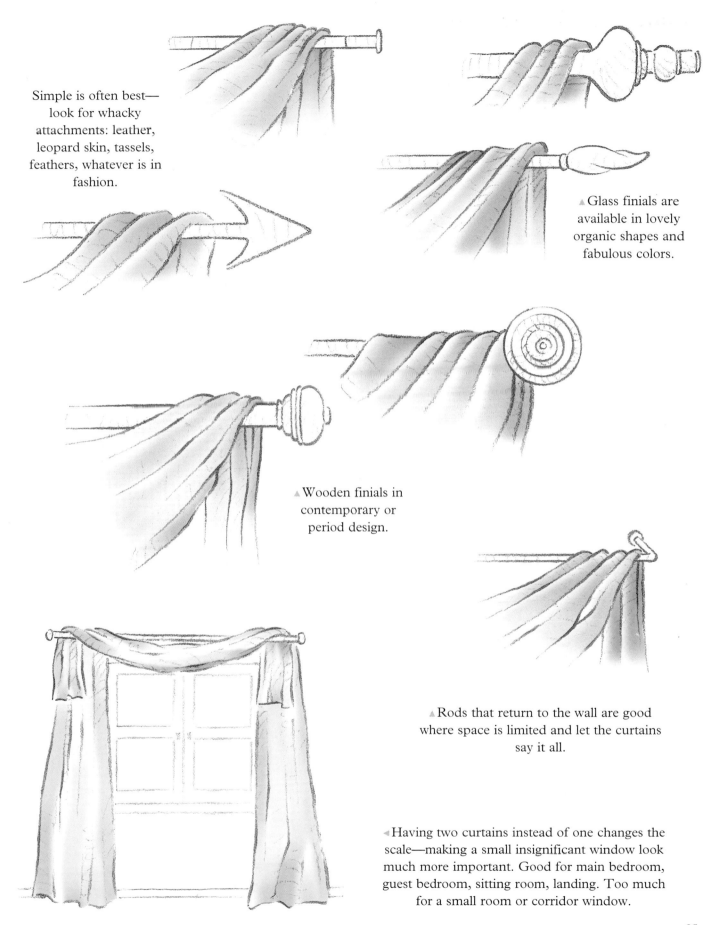

Simple is often best—look for whacky attachments: leather, leopard skin, tassels, feathers, whatever is in fashion.

▲ Glass finials are available in lovely organic shapes and fabulous colors.

▲ Wooden finials in contemporary or period design.

▲ Rods that return to the wall are good where space is limited and let the curtains say it all.

◂ Having two curtains instead of one changes the scale—making a small insignificant window look much more important. Good for main bedroom, guest bedroom, sitting room, landing. Too much for a small room or corridor window.

Swags and Tails

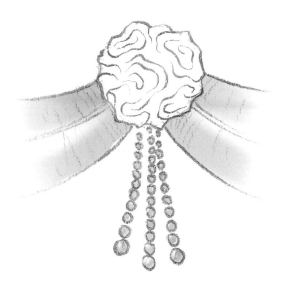

◄ Match the swag size to the window widths.

▲ Rosettes, choux, or floral corsages punctuate the swags.

◄ Draping the swag over the tails makes the window appear taller. Decorate with looped cord and tassels.

► Swags and tails are traditional, elegant top treatments for formal windows. High ceilings, a beautiful room and stunning furnishings are essential prerequisites.

▲ High ceilinged bay windows can take the simplest or the most complex top treatments, arrangements and finishes.

► There is no strict rule covering the positioning and lengths of tails—look up text book treatments and make sketches of your own window to guide your decision.

Swags and Tails Gallery

For a more contemporary look, leave out the tails and finish the swags with the same fabric or something original. Keep the fabrics light, bouncy and light-reflecting—any kind of silk or silk and wool mix.

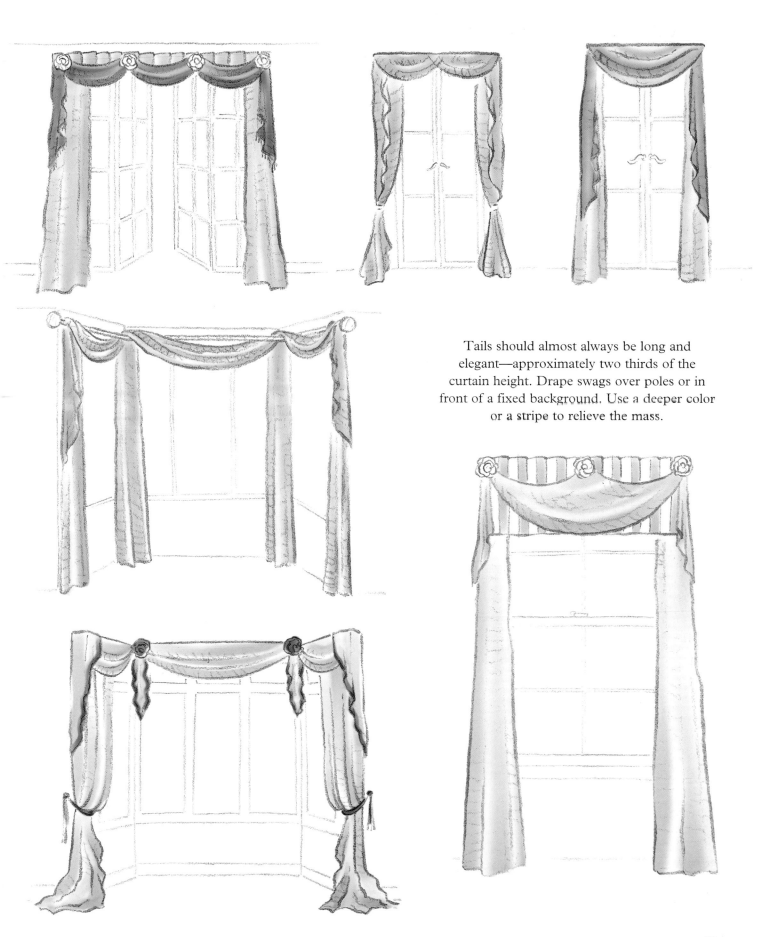

Tails should almost always be long and elegant—approximately two thirds of the curtain height. Drape swags over poles or in front of a fixed background. Use a deeper color or a stripe to relieve the mass.

Soft Cornices

Soft cornices, where the fabric is not closely fitted to a cornice board, are preferred for bedrooms, nurseries and where the walls and ceilings are uneven. And for most rooms of informal homes, such as a country cottage.

◄Personalize with a machine or hand-stitched motif or initial.

◄Always have long curtains with top treatments. To get the best proportions, make a paper or fabric template first and pin to the wall above the window.

◄Always adapt any design to follow the structure of the window. If you have two or more different windows in one room, design a treatment which will work equally well with each.

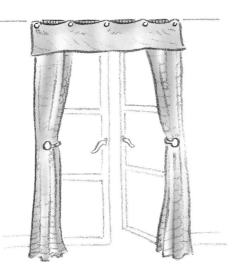

◀ Buttons and buttonholes are one way to fix—other ideas could be to use ties, studs, eyelets or pins.

▲ Very easy to make and effective: cover the wooden board with fabric and fix a flat piece of fabric at intervals, allowing it to drop a little between fixings. Where a door opens inward, be careful of the cornice length.

▶ Simple gathered valances work in most windows and for most situations where there is something to cover up but where the valance doesn't need or want to be the main feature. Here a self-colored fringe softens and finishes the lower edge.

Soft Cornice Gallery

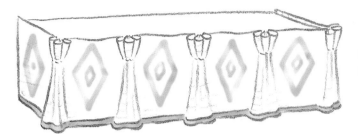

◄ Plan triple pleats evenly across, with one facing forwards at each corner.

► Inverted box pleats, choose a contrast fabric to go behind.

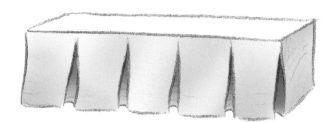

◄ Goblet pleats are finished with cord knotted at the base of each.

► Pencil pleats hold the fullness neatly against the board, fan edging softens the lower edge.

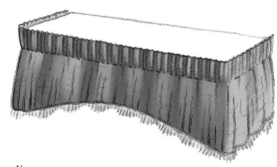

◄ Frilled headings can stand above the board, knotted cords create a strong line.

► Bunched headings are informal, also good against uneven ceilings.

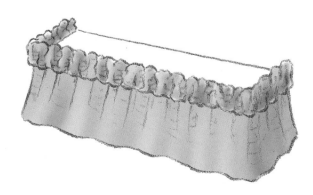

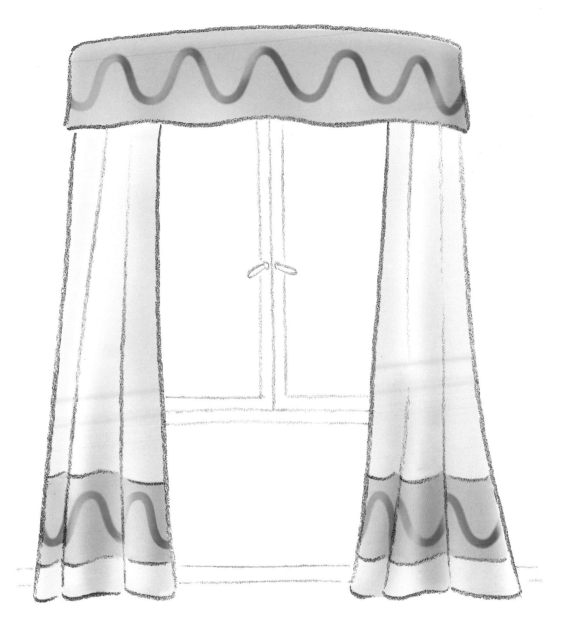

▲A wide border for the cornice and at the bottom of the curtains makes a strong statement, drawing attention away from a very boring window.

▼A good traditional shape
for a tall window.

▼Cut the cornice as high as possible in the center to gain maximum light.

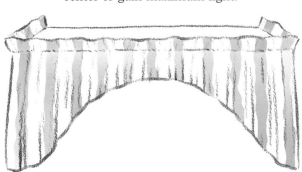

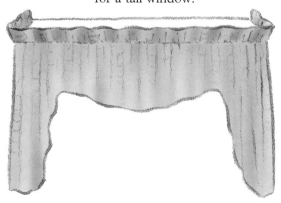

Hard Cornices

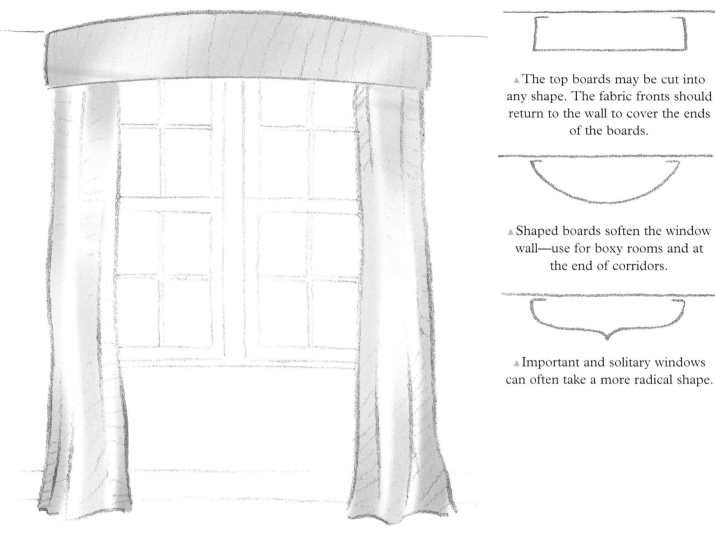

▲ The top boards may be cut into any shape. The fabric fronts should return to the wall to cover the ends of the boards.

▲ Shaped boards soften the window wall—use for boxy rooms and at the end of corridors.

▲ Important and solitary windows can often take a more radical shape.

Shape the bottom edges and decorate the front of cornices in simple or contemporary finishes.

◄ Traditional painted and gilded cornices are most suited for formal windows, but can on occasion be used to dress up a simple window.

▼ Gilded or painted metal or carved wooden top pieces formalize a soft, draped cornice.

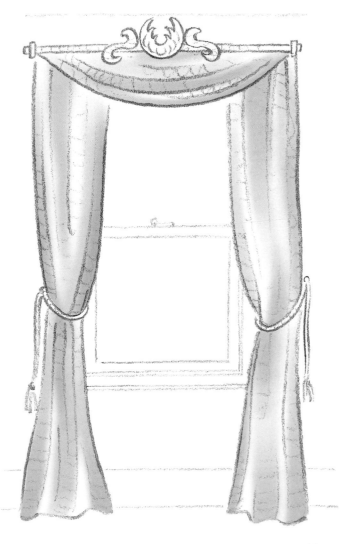

Choose cornices firstly because they are the window treatment which best complements the house and the room. Other factors which might influence the need for a cornice are—pipes above the window, a deep dead light, a gap in the cornice, an uneven ceiling, the need for a feature, to cover the fittings of multi-layered coverings.

Lambrequin: Bay and Moroccan

Traditionally, lambrequin are tapestry panels worked and fitted around the window to decorate. Shutters which folded over the windows against the night also provided security and draft proofing. Sheer curtains behind the lambrequin protected flooring and furniture from direct sunlight.

An original take on an old idea—a stunning frame to surround a boring doorway, entrance, corridor or room divider. The Moorish shape is fun and easily adapts to almost any size of opening.

Lambrequin: Contemporary

Simply cut wooden boards frame recessed sash windows in a children's room. Roller shades from behind pull down to cover the window. Naive painting, stencilling or postcards and cut-out shapes make these individual.

This is fun for a small child to decorate using poster paints—a few strokes out of place won't matter.

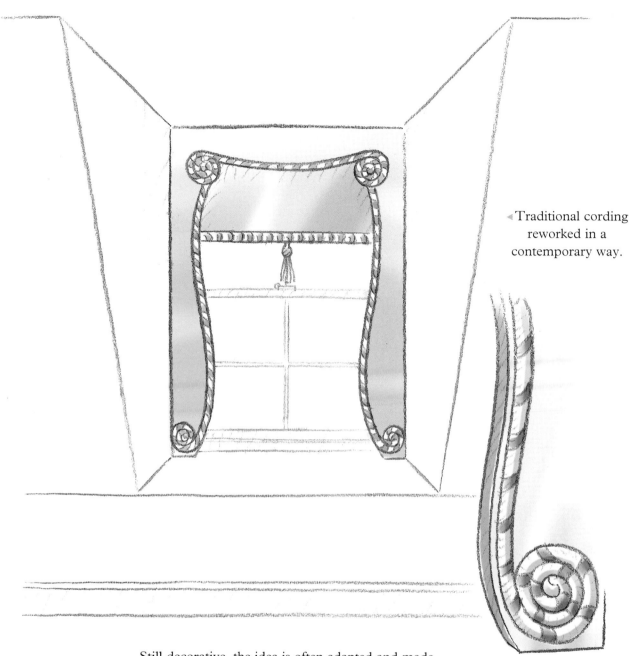

◂Traditional cording
reworked in a
contemporary way.

Still decorative, the idea is often adapted and made
from wood, painted or stencilled or covered with
fabric. Good for hiding the unattractive fittings of
roller shades and covering up the ugly edges of
some windows. Small windows benefit from a
structured treatment with a shade behind, taking
minimal light. These really are things you can do
yourself and have fun with.

Tiebacks: Informal

Tiebacks can hold curtains back in more or less formal manner depending on the treatment.

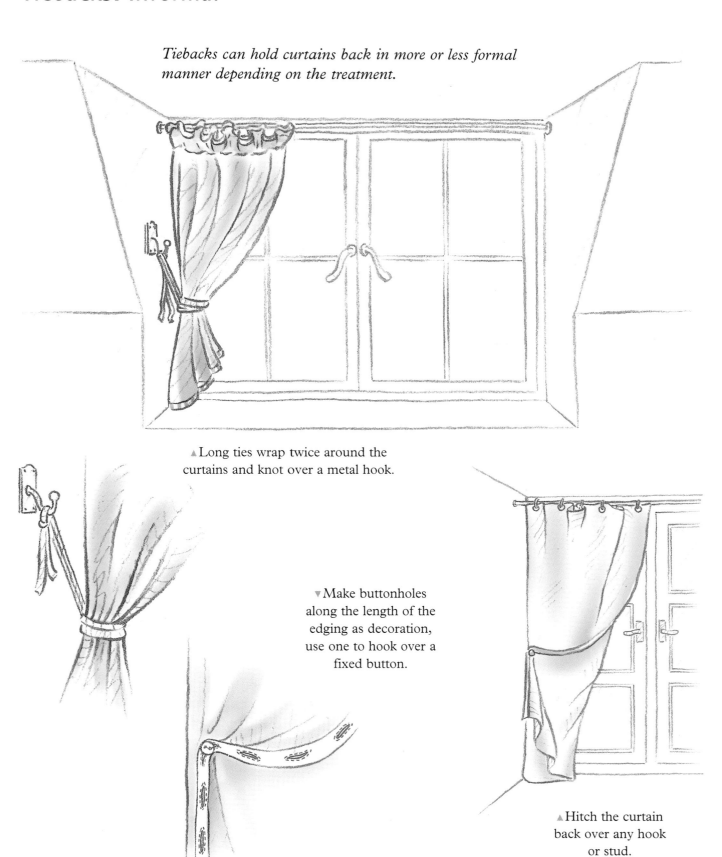

▲Long ties wrap twice around the curtains and knot over a metal hook.

▼Make buttonholes along the length of the edging as decoration, use one to hook over a fixed button.

▲Hitch the curtain back over any hook or stud.

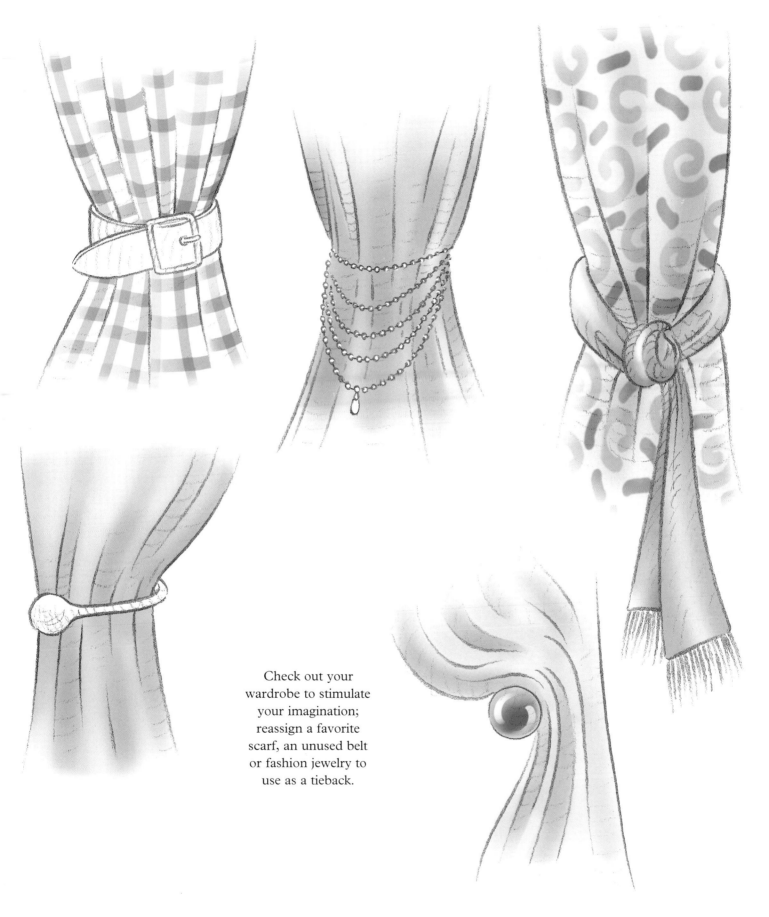

Check out your
wardrobe to stimulate
your imagination;
reassign a favorite
scarf, an unused belt
or fashion jewelry to
use as a tieback.

Tiebacks: Formal

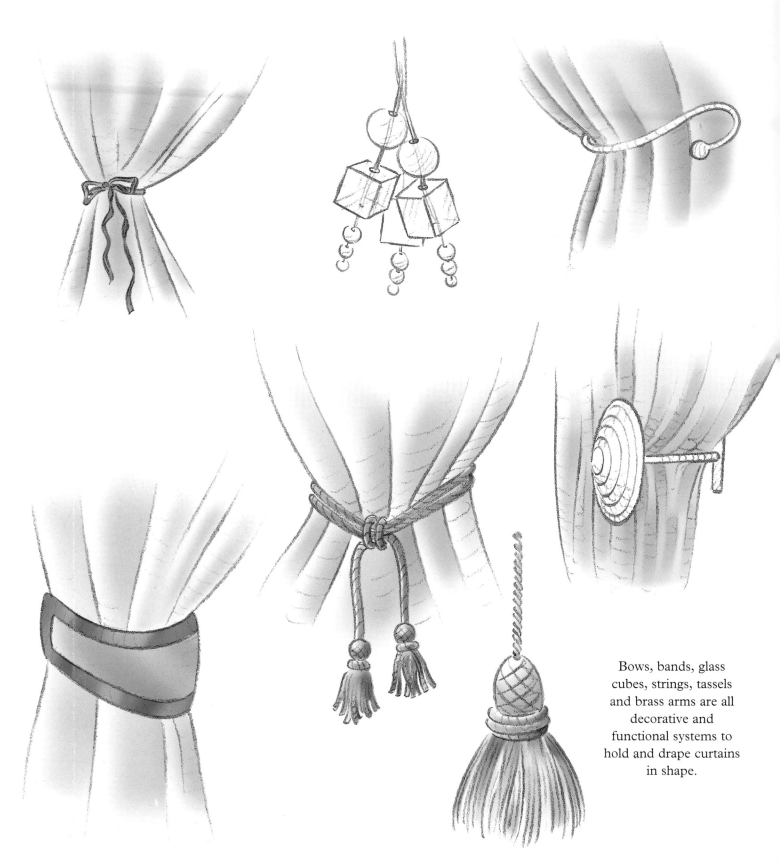

Bows, bands, glass cubes, strings, tassels and brass arms are all decorative and functional systems to hold and drape curtains in shape.

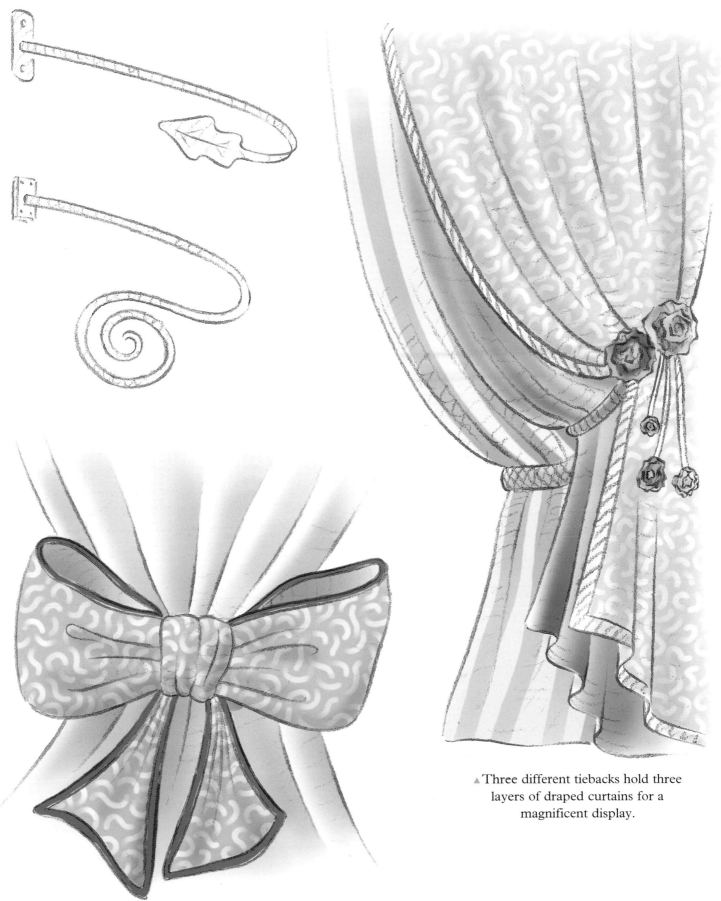

▲ Three different tiebacks hold three
layers of draped curtains for a
magnificent display.

Tiebacks Gallery

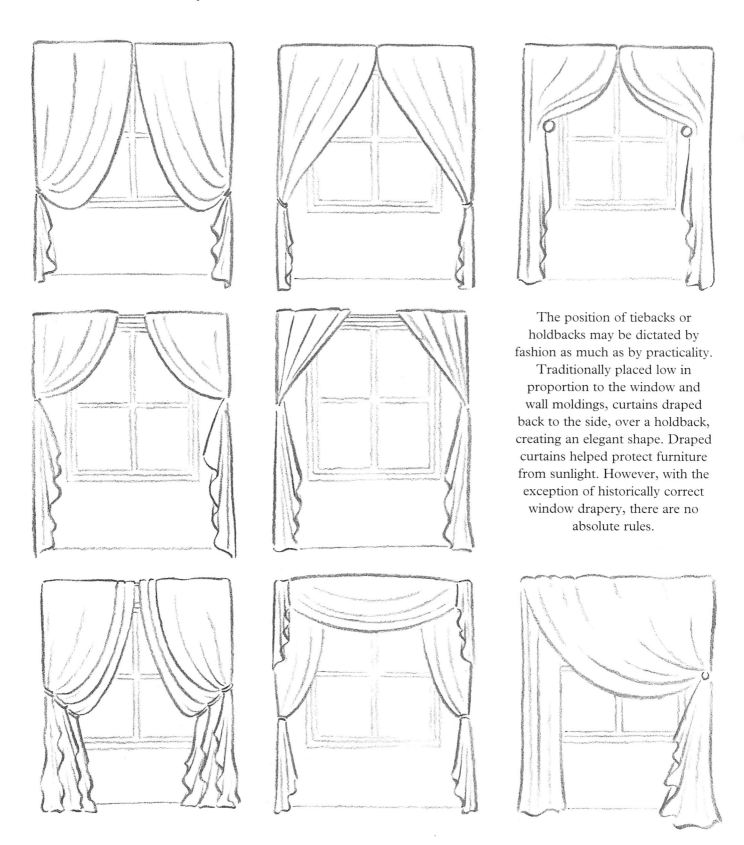

The position of tiebacks or holdbacks may be dictated by fashion as much as by practicality. Traditionally placed low in proportion to the window and wall moldings, curtains draped back to the side, over a holdback, creating an elegant shape. Draped curtains helped protect furniture from sunlight. However, with the exception of historically correct window drapery, there are no absolute rules.

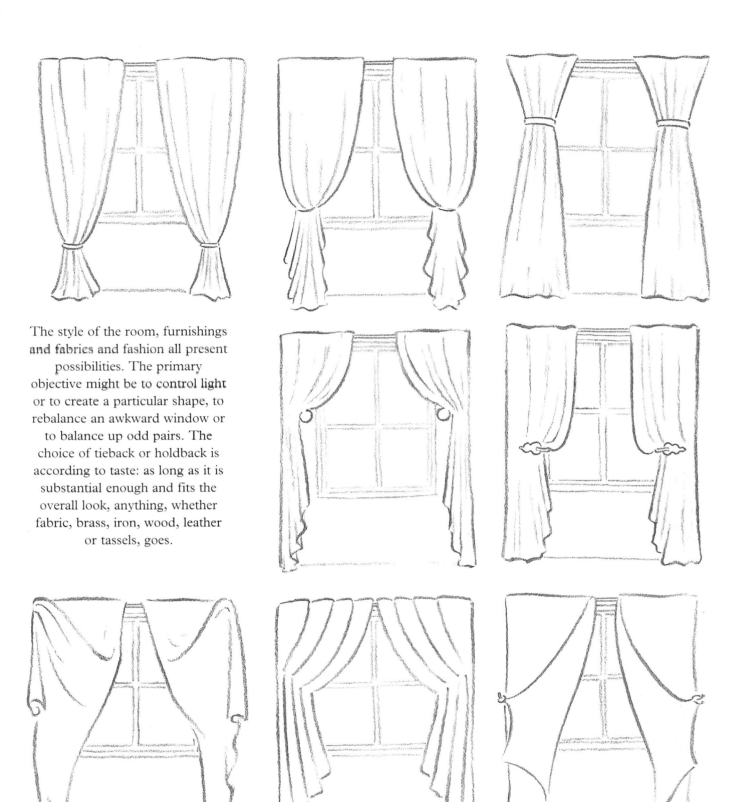

The style of the room, furnishings and fabrics and fashion all present possibilities. The primary objective might be to control light or to create a particular shape, to rebalance an awkward window or to balance up odd pairs. The choice of tieback or holdback is according to taste: as long as it is substantial enough and fits the overall look, anything, whether fabric, brass, iron, wood, leather or tassels, goes.

PROBLEM SOLVING

Unusual Windows

Some of the most interesting windows, from an architectural point of view, are also the most difficult to curtain. To spoil the shape would be a travesty, so where there is no need to cover, leave well alone. However, if the window is situated in a bedroom or bathroom, privacy may be required, so some direction is offered here. Whatever you choose should perform the necessary function without altering the shape of the window from the outside. Any of the ideas illustrated can be adapted to any of these shaped window frames.

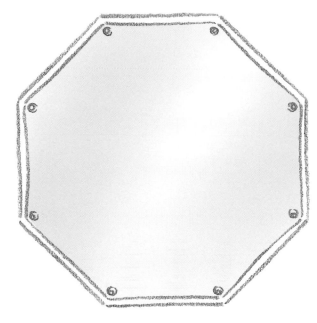

Octagonal
Perhaps the simplest covering to make is a flat fabric panel. This should be the shape of the window, with loops at intervals sympathetic to the frame, which can be clipped in place to cover. To take down, either remove, fold and store close by, or fold down on itself so that the bottom part remains in place.

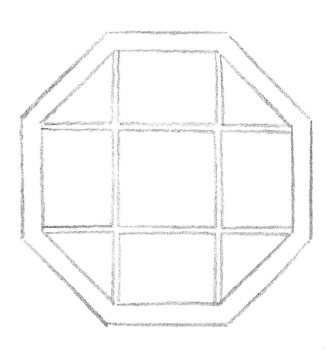

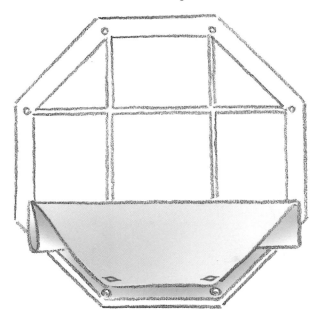

Garden Rooms

Unless you are overlooked, these windows are best left uncovered. If you feel some decoration is wanted, colored glass, etched glass, semi-permanent artworks or candles burning at night should provide enough interest. However, if you are overlooked, or just prefer to cover the darkness, flat fabric panels or pierced screens can be fixed into or onto the window. Moroccan-style grilles can be made from perforated wood or metal sheets cut to fit each window. Fix simple catches at top and bottom to secure or push tightly in place with a central knob.

Round

For complete coverage, full-sized "stops" or "plugs" can be made to fit snugly inside any window frame—either in solid wood, painted, or covered in a suitable material such as faux suede or leather, or a wooden frame with fabric stretched over, rather like a flattish umbrella. Make as attractive as possible, so that it looks interesting when it is stored, preferably somewhere close to the window.

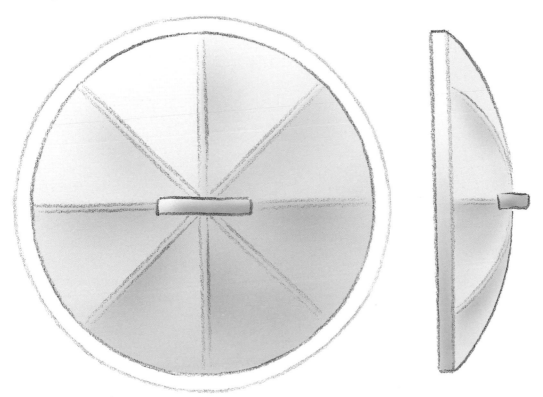

Unusual and Difficult Windows

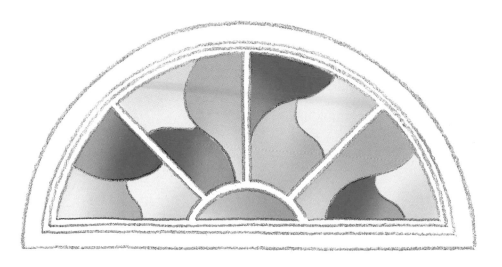

Colored glass
Colored glazing—in either contemporary or traditional design and color—will give permanent privacy, let pretty light into the room when the sun shines, and at the same time, disguise the darkness of night.

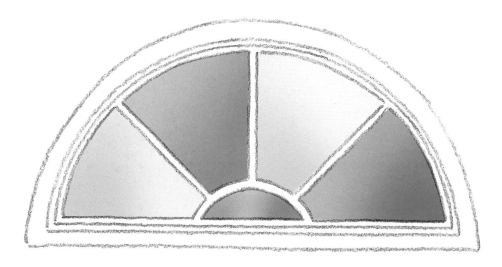

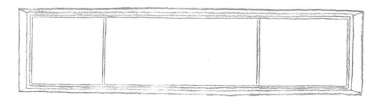

Uneven pairs of windows
These come in all sorts of shapes and sizes, usually as a result of later alteration. If yours are well-proportioned, treat them as a single unit. If they are ill-proportioned, you will need to choose between treating them so that they do end up looking similar or treating them completely differently.

You can use furniture to visually balance diverse windows. For example, placing a bookcase close to a tall window will make it look wider, a chest or side table sited below a higher window will take the eye to the ground. Use lamps or tall vases and picture frames to bridge any wall gap. In each of these cases the more normal window would have long curtains and the other window would either be dressed to match or given a Roman shade.

You might choose roller or Roman shades to match the walls, with long dress curtains. When the shades are closed, the shape of the dress curtains dominate.

High clerestory windows
These tend to be ugly and situated to gain additional light with little regard to pleasing the eye, often either side of a fireplace, but sometimes in a long corridor or close to a solid door. My preference is always to dress them as simply as possible, either with a shade or flat curtain which is unobtrusive by day. Always in the same color as the surrounding wall, and, if at all possible, in the same material.

Grilles

A grille of pierced metal can be made to fit any shape of window and held in place with clips. The beauty of this covering is that it really can be lifted on and off easily, and an attractive piece can be decoratively propped against or hung on the wall close by. If it is left in place, interesting patterns of light will be created.

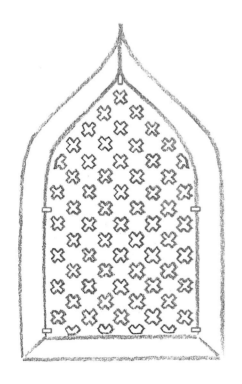

Slit windows

If you have long, narrow windows, make the most of them. The degree and angle of light received is a bonus and the benefit out of all proportion to the window size with shafts of constantly changing light and shade falling quietly across walls, furniture and floors. If you need to cover, then use a grille or tiny slatted blind hidden at the top, so that the light may still enter in a controlled way.

Better still, although in many ways a "non-solution", would be to stand a tall glass sculpture in the recess which will allow the light to filter through without blocking and, at the same time, provide some degree of privacy. Or at night, burn a chunky church candle, perhaps with a glass cover to enhance the light and for safety.

The flickering light against the darkness outside provides all the decoration a simple window needs.

Radiators

Radiators located under a window are always a hindrance to elegance and good proportion. If the heat given is non-essential, then dress the window regardless. For bedrooms you could cover deep sills with inconspicuous vents and short skirts which fall almost to the floor.

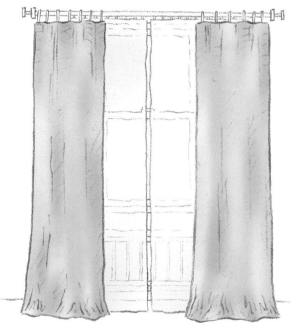

▲ If the radiator sill projects into the room, deep cornices or extended pole brackets can hold the curtains further forwards than normal.

▲ Make a deep window seat, cushion the top and allow curtains to fall informally.

▲ Make a feature with grilled
sides and top, with shades to
cover the window.

▲ If you need the heat from the radiator, short
curtains might be alright in a bedroom or landing
but, for a formal room, use thick shades to cover
the window until the room is warm enough for
curtains to be pulled or draped over.

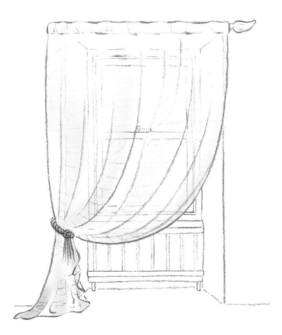

▲ Where some heat is desirable, use sheers on poles
which allow heat through and up, or leave the radiator
on low, then cover with thick curtains.

An Ugly Outlook

Windows are the eyes of the house—essential to the good proportion outside and to provide light inside. It is to be expected and hoped that the view from any window will provide an extra dimension by providing a focal point outside the room. Sadly, especially in built-up areas where light and privacy are most necessary, inappropriate and unsympathetic building works have denied either one or both. In these cases it has to be enough to gain as much light as possible while turning the focal point of the room inward.

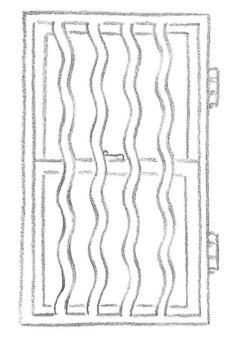

▲Sheer fabric coverings are one answer, as are Moorish-style, pierced grilles, colored glass and even mirrored panes.

◄Or use the window recess to fix shelves for books or other collections, perhaps incorporating these as deep shelves into a full-height unit. As long as the window frame is disguised by the bookcase frame, no one will ever know about the ugly window behind.

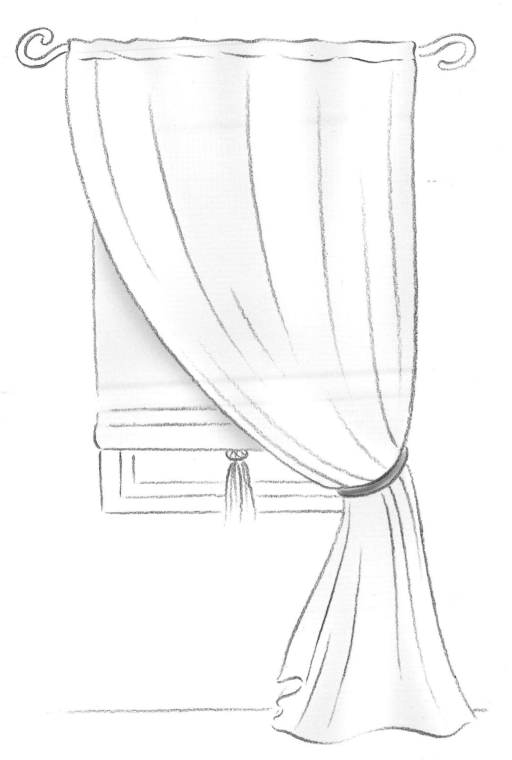

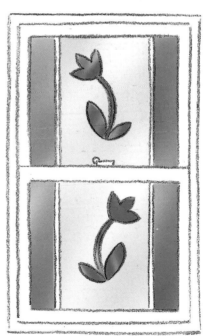

▼Find or commission a stained glass window and if necessary supplement the available light outside by artificial means. It might be appropriate to paint a false window with a false view and slot in place, obscuring the light altogether and relying on top lighting or uplighting from inside.

▲Partially ugly scenes outside can be cleverly disguised much more easily. Use shutters or half-shutters, drape one or two curtains across as low as needed, keep shades lowered, hang cornices or lambrequin frames.

FACTS AND FIGURES

FABRICS

It is not the purpose of this book to give any particular direction as to which fabric you must choose, in which color and scale for which window treatment: only to suggest where some sort of pattern or geometric prints or weaves might be used or mixed together. Fashion changes in furnishing fabrics and colors preclude strict advice for these curtain sketches, which suggest and inspire rather than rigidly dictate.

Type

All window treatments will work with plain fabrics, especially those with an interesting weave or inherent sheen which will throw the light. The important elements are texture, weight and color. The weight, or "hand" of a fabric, is crucial to the end result and must do the job for which it is intended, whether you want thick draft stoppers or light, floaty drapes. Always handle a decent-sized piece of fabric so that you can see and feel the drape and weight and how it hangs. For instance, wool might be heavy enough but too springy for your use, or muslin light enough but too see-through.

Consider fabrics which are widely available but may not be found on the shelves of soft furnishings shops. Most dressmaking fabrics will stand up to light furnishing use, but may not like direct sunlight. Ginghams, crushed velvets, cotton prints and silk noiles are all inexpensive and can look stunning if used either for full curtains or for flat panels with good detailing. Try unusual fabrics, such as table felts, woven plaids, faux leather, faux suede, real leather and suede, or kelims and other antique rugs, blankets or sheets or lengths of tweed or shirting cotton from factory outlets.

Color

An expanse of solid-colored fabric will benefit from an interesting texture or a small geometric print to relieve the plainness without distracting from the shape. Neutral colors—sand, oyster, beige, corn, buttermilk, rye—are always possible and often the best choice. Curtains are expensive, so if you want a more dramatic color, it may be better to add it to the walls using inexpensive pots of paint. Whatever the color chosen, select a fabric with a good weave which has movement and interest. Check that the color doesn't go completely dead on a dull day, and plan evening lighting so that some indirect light washes onto the curtains.

If you want color or are in love with a particular print, go for softer tones in colors which you feel the most comfortable with. Harsh colors can be difficult to add to and furnish around. Save fashion colors for accessory items such as cushions, and impact colors for specific areas where the furnishings will inevitably have a relatively short life, such as garden rooms and playrooms.

Most decorating disasters are made from trying too hard, perhaps including too many colors or patterns in too many colors, or in playing too safe with boring, flat colors. Unless you are a designer, an artist or experienced decorator and know well how to break the rules, choose one fabric at a time and then add others. For a simple elegant result, have the first fabric in one basic color, then add others in the same color but with variations of tone and pattern. Or try using two close plain colors and adding prints or weaves combining tones of both. You will need to introduce splashes of other, opposite colors if the room is to stay alive. These can be added to suit your budget and thoughtfully, as cushions, paintings, flowers or trimmings.

Composition

Natural fibers—wool, cotton, linen and silk in any combination, weave or print—are well proven to last and clean well. Some synthetic element may be needed if your curtains have to be fire retardant but, as a general rule, the qualities of natural materials will far outweigh any synthetic alternative. Having said that, there are some very good silk look-alikes which don't rot and fade at the window, that do have a place. Look for some of the more interesting fabrics being developed, e.g. where pure fiber, such as grasses or banana leaves, have been woven into silks and cotton sheers.

WHICH WINDOW TREATMENT?

Consider your room and general style of architecture and furniture. Do you want a traditional or a more contemporary look? As you make your choice, consider how long you are likely to be in the same house: your curtains will usually outlast other furniture and may well still be at that window or recycled to another in ten or twenty years' time. If you move a lot or intend to move, it can make equal sense either a) to make overlong and overfull so that one pair of curtains can be used many times or b) to make as economically as possible both in cost and design to minimize potential waste.

CURTAIN STYLE CHECKLIST

Consider these options:

Practically:

i) do you want heavy or light curtains, unlined, lined or interlined?
ii) do you need to keep the dark out at night?
iii) do you need partial or complete privacy?
iv) how well insulated is the house itself: how cold will it be in the worst weather; do you have howling drafts and winds?
v) do you need to protect from strong sunlight?
vi) are there obstacles to accommodate/overcome?

Stylistically:

i) how elegant or informal is the room?
ii) how much color and/or texture and pattern do you want?
iii) how full and what sort of headings?
iv) how long should they be?
v) is there something to hide/disguise?
vi) does the proportion of the window need to be altered, improved?

Economically:

i) how much can you afford to spend right now?
ii) how long are they likely to last?
iii) do you prefer to have a lot of fullness and therefore quantity at less cost per yard?
iv) have you chosen a very expensive fabric: it could be used flat or combined with more of a middle cost fabric?
v) are you trying to revamp curtaining from a previous home?

And perhaps most importantly of all, how experienced are you with a needle, how much space do you have to work in, and how much work do you want to do toward it? If you are unsure, select a good-natured fabric without a pattern repeat and simple curtaining. Masses of inexpensive fabric in overlong curtains can hide a multitude of poor stitches, whereas the simple looking flat panels do need to be absolutely accurate if they are to hang and pull effectively and professionally. If you want to make flat panels, choose a fabric which holds itself up, e.g. faux suede, and if you want light elegant drapes, choose silk or soft wool challis.

SHADES AND SHEERS

Even when you have a tremendous view which is the focal point of your room, light entering through any window is improved if it is filtered or controlled. The most effective ways are with shades or lightweight, sheer curtains.

Shades very successfully direct daylight to enter the room low, sheers filter and direct light lengthwise. To test which you prefer, sacrifice the sky, by part covering the top of the window for a couple of days and notice how much softer the light is and how different the room looks. If you eat or work close to a sunny window, shades can make life more comfortable. As the sun moves around, they can be raised and lowered by small degrees and with minimum fuss, individually or all at the same time.

If you have a radiator underneath a window, shades are fairly essential coverings. Fitted with or without curtains, shades allow the radiator to function effectively in cold weather. Padded shades covering the whole window and sitting on, or just in front of, the sill are almost as effective as heavy curtains.

Rolled Shades

Rolled shades take time to furl and unfurl, are very informal and soften hard windows, whereas Roman shades are more formal, as each pleat is held straight with a metal or wooden rod behind. Rolled shades can be positioned in a formal, even manner or randomly, each pulled to a different height and none straight. The rolled edges make these shades attractive to look at from the side, an important consideration when dressing a square bay, or a window positioned to the side of the entrance to a room. They are good for where daylight needs to be controlled but the windows never completely covered. An outlook over a city nightscape would be an ideal situation.

Roman Shades

Roman shades can be operated independently within each window section to work with outside light and inside activity. So they are especially good for bay windows and for any window where the individual sections are clearly defined. Stripes look really effective, but they can be difficult to work with unless the fabric is very straight and tightly woven. Bold patterns are seen to their best advantage with this style of shade. Plain fabrics need some sort of edging unless the design brief is that they discreetly disappear into the background.

Roller Shades

Roller shades are ugly if used alone in a window as the fittings are not attractive. The sides don't fit close to the sides of the window recess, so they are always best used with curtains which cover the sides of the windows. But they are flat and operate easily, fulfilling the twin criteria of filtering and directing light, with impunity.

LAYERS

Where a multi-layered design has been chosen, either select fabrics which need to be seen through each other, or add a lining to at least one of the layers. Linings can be in the same color as the top fabric, so the actual colors are unchanged. Of course, there are many times when layers are chosen with the sole intention that the various colors and tones will interact with each other, so that the whole effect depends on this chemistry. You could still line the undermost layer with a fine lawn, light enough that daylight is barely filtered—the effect will remain unspoiled and all fabrics will be protected.

LIGHT

Usually the more light we can get the better. However there are times and situations where the amount of light should be controlled or at least filtered. Sunlight streaming in through a large window can ruin valuable furniture, bleach sofa covers and carpets and damage curtains. Bright light may also disturb work at a desk or table close to the window, or the viewing of a computer or television screen. Shades of lightweight Holland fabric which pull down, both control and filter the light. Sheer curtains behind top curtains can be drawn across easily to cover the whole or part of the window.

You may need to block artificial light at night. If your bedroom window is close to an annoying street light, you might want to block the outside entirely with heavy interlined curtains or woven damasks. Layers of mixed fabrics can provide for all needs—perhaps faux suede, wool or other dense material at the top with sheer fabrics nearest the window. Combinations of flat panels, curtains or curtains and shades can all be designed to suit.

PRIVACY

Complete privacy is only possible by entirely covering the window. This you can do with shades or curtains, or full, sheer under-curtains. If there is light on at night, then only thick curtains or solid shades will provide exclusion. Partial privacy is much easier. Light curtains, unlined shades, almost-meeting flat panels or wood-slatted blinds will all cover the window completely to give visual protection while still allowing plenty of daylight through. Any layered window treatment can be designed to accommodate many levels of block-out. It may be that a curtain can be draped in such a way as to provide all the cover you require, without the need to keep opening and closing curtains or shades.

NOISE

Double-glazed windowpanes eliminate most outside sound, which is fine when windows are closed, but not if you prefer to leave them open. How you deal with this will largely depend on your window or location. You could fit a heavy shade close to the glass, but there isn't always the room and many windows are unsuitable, for instance, if shutters close across inside or if light is at a premium.

Heavy fabrics absorb sound extremely effectively and with substantial interlining you can create an effective sound barrier. If you have a problem with general or specific noise, the thicker and heavier you make the curtains, the better. Curtains might not help you in the day, but can improve life in the evenings and early mornings when you are trying to sleep, relax or socialize. If you need to sleep in the daytime and like to have air flowing through open windows, the thickest, darkest possible curtains can be lifesavers. Although thick curtains are often chosen to prevent drafts completely, an open window behind drawn curtains will provide enough gentle movement for air to filter through in a refreshing, rather than intrusive, way.

SHEERS

If you like to wake with light cheering up your bedroom, sheer curtains let you do so gradually and calmly. Many lightweight and open-weave fabrics can be used for sheer curtains, and many are washable, which is a great bonus. You can use linen scrim (the sort used to clean windows)—it's a sort of sacking color, so you look straight through it and it's invisible from the outside. Muslin is good, use butter muslin if your budget is very tight, but if you can afford it, buy the finest quality, which is almost a lawn voile. Almost any lightweight textile is suitable: linen voile, cotton organdy, silk organza, cotton lawn, silk habutai, taffeta and, occasionally, a fine wool challis. The best colors are off-white or natural unless you want to make a statement from outside as well as inside.

If the sheers are for privacy, use at least three times fullness—anything less and the view to the inside is only partially obscured. If they are mainly for softness in the room and to filter the light, then anything over double fullness is fine.

LINING

Curtains are lined for practicality, to protect the top fabric from sunlight and condensation, and also for appearance. Condensation and strong sunlight will discolor and eventually rot any curtain fabric, so it's better to replace the lining than the curtain. Linings may enhance the look of the curtain fabric, deepening the colors, or adding a little bulk. Sateen curtain lining is a treated fabric designed expressly for the purpose and it's worth buying the best. Occasionally patterned linings form part of the window treatment, especially where curtains may be turned around at the hem or draped back in such a manner as to show the linings.

INTERLINING

Interlined curtains just look so different from lined or unlined curtains that the decision to interline or not is as likely to be influenced as much or more by the wish for the look of thick, heavy curtains as for the need of them.

There are four main reasons to interline curtains: to improve the drape of a fine fabric; to absorb annoying sound; to catch the weather's worst; and to make a room as dark as possible. If you need and want thick curtains, they might as well be long and luxurious, falling in generous folds. Just choose an interesting but uncomplicated fabric, and if you want to jazz it up, add some breathtaking tiebacks or stitch cords and fringes onto the finished curtain.

PLANNING AND MEASURING CURTAINS

The most successful window treatments are those that have been carefully considered and designed from the start. It can be helpful to make a scale drawing of the whole wall or walls, particularly when there are windows of different sizes or designs in the same room. Experimenting on paper will give you a feel for what works best. Playing with the length of the curtains and combinations of curtains, cornices and tiebacks, as well as considering the scale and proportion of windows in relation to the room, will suggest ideas for design and show up what works and what doesn't.

Take accurate window measurements, using a metal or wooden rule, as described below. Round them up or down to the nearest $\frac{1}{4}$" (6 mm) and transfer them to graph paper. Work with a very simple scale, say, 1" = 10" or 1 cm = 10 cm, and mark the room height, the window position and space around. Mark any potential obstacles, such as pipes, beams, radiators and anything outside which you would prefer not to see. Don't worry if you have no previous drawing experience, the most rudimentary of lines will be of some help. Photocopy one or more of the sketches from the book and scale up or down to make it as close to your window size as possible. Copy the window wall onto tracing paper and clip over the photocopies to see how the ideas work.

Once you have a fairly definite concept, make some marks on the wall and pin newspaper or old sheets into place to see how the proportions look. Stand back and check for any ugly fittings, such as unsightly double glazing or window bars. You may want to add shades, or position tiebacks to cover something up or make a new shape. If you want a top treatment, make a template and tack it into position to check how it will look.

Measure the width and height of the window in at least three places to make sure that you have accounted for floor or ceiling slopes and whether or not the window is square.

ACCURATE MEASUREMENTS

Take the following measurements:
▲ From the top of the frame or reveal to the floor
▲ From the ceiling to the top of the window
▲ From the ceiling to the floor
▲ The window width inside, noting any obstacles, such as telephone jacks
▲ The window width outside
▲ The distance available to the sides of the window for the curtain stack-back.

For curtains to hang outside reveal

The following measurements are required:
1 Width of window
2 Width of stack-back
3 Top of frame to ceiling
4 Top of frame to sill
5 Top of frame to below sill
6 Top of frame to floor
7 Ceiling to floor

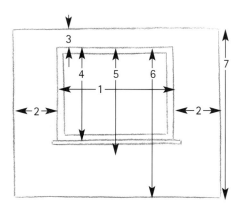

For curtains to hang inside reveal

The following measurements are required:
1 Width inside frame
2 Length from top of window to sill
3 Depth of frame

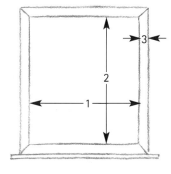
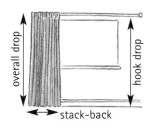

ESTIMATING CURTAIN FABRIC

The amount of fabric you need for each window is relative to the style of curtaining that you wish to make. The three factors to bear in mind are: the fullness, the length and the heading style. You will have already chosen your window treatment and from this you will know the fittings width and overall drop of the curtains. Make allowances for any proposed alterations to the room for instance, cupboards to be fitted close to the window or a change of flooring.

Fullness

The fullness of curtains dictates the number of widths or part widths of fabric needed for each curtain. Most curtains look best with at least double fullness, i.e. twice the width of the window area, but this may be reduced for short curtains that do not need the weight to hang well. If the stack-back space is restricted, pleated headings will hold the curtain back into the smallest space. Allow only 1¼ to 1½ times fullness if you have a dominant and special design that needs to be seen.

Heading	Fullness
gathered	double for heavy fabrics, two-and-a-half to three time for voiles
bunched	two-and-a-quarter to three times
smocked	depending on your pattern – make a small sample first, allow three times
pencil-pleated	two-and-a-quarter to three times
hand-pleated	triple and goblets: two-and-a-half to three times

Fabric widths

Use the following example to estimate the number of curtain widths you will need. Measure the track or pole.

1 Pole/track width for two curtains   72" (183 cm)
    divide by 2 for width of one curtain   36" (91.5 cm)
    for side return add   3½" (9 cm)
    for center overlap add   3½" (9 cm)
    total   43" (109 cm)
2 Multiply by the required fullness
    43" (109 cm) × 2.5   107½" (274 cm)
3 Divide by the width of your fabric.
    107½" ÷ 54" (274 ÷ 137 cm)   1.99
4 Each curtain will need 2 widths fabric

Length

There are three critical measurements:

1 the overall drop, which is the finished length of the curtain;

2 the hook drop, which is the length from the fitting ring or loop to the desired length;

3 the cutting length including heading and hem allowances. Also including allowances for pattern repeat— see later.

The hook drop is straightforward and can be obtained as soon as the fittings are in place. The overall drop is the hook drop plus the heading above. The cutting length is the overall drop plus heading and hem allowances.

Headings

From the sketches chosen you will know whether the headings will be informal or formal, and you will need to include enough fabric in the cutting length for your heading. Plan any pattern or stripe to fit sympathetically at the top of the heading.

Heading	Allowance
gathered	add the depth of frill above the hook drop and back down behind the tape.
bunched	add at least four times the depth of the "bunch" to the hook drop
pencil-pleated	add the depth of the pleats to the overall drop
pocket headings	add twice the depth of the pocket to the overall drop
bound headings	no allowance needed above the overall drop
smocked	add the depth of the smocking pattern to the overall drop
goblet/triple pleats	add twice the depth of the pleat to the overall drop

Hems

You need enough to hide the raw edges, to give the curtains weight and to allow for possible eventual alteration. The following allowances are comfortable and workable, you may use a little more but not less. These are all added to the overall drop.

Hem	Allowance
unlined curtains	8" (20.5 cm) for double hem
lined curtains	8" (20.5 cm) for double hem
bound hems	no extra fabric
interlined curtains	4" (10 cm) for single hem
voile curtains	3" (7.5 cm) for double hem

Cutting length

Use the following example for full-length curtains as a guide to calculating the amount of fabric needed for each curtain length.

1   Overall drop ceiling to floor   108" (274.5 cm)
   less ¾" (2 cm) carpet allowance   107¼" (272.5 cm)
   less ¾" (2 cm) cornice allowance   106½" (270.5 cm)
   plus 2" (5 cm) extra drop length   108½" (275.5 cm)

2   Add 8" (20.5 cm) hem allowance   116¼" (290 cm)
   Add 8" (20.5 cm) heading allowance   124½" (316 cm)

3   Each cut length is   124½" (316 cm)

Pattern repeat

You will need to make sure that each cut length will pattern match to the next. The quickest way to do this is to add one whole pattern repeat to each cutting length. However, this might be wasteful and it follows that it could also be expensive. So just add enough that each length will fit into multiples of the pattern repeat.

1 If you take the first route, assuming the pattern repeat is 27" (68.5 cm), the cutting length will be:
   124½" + 27" = 151½" (316 cm + 68.5 cm = 385 cm), this amount will produce the most waste

2 If you take the second option, you need to divide the total cutting length by the length of the pattern repeat, then round it up:
   124½" ÷ 27" = 4.6 (316 cm ÷ 68.5 cm = 4.6)
   Round up to 5.
   5 × 27" (68.5 cm) = 135" (343 cm), required for each curtain, then add a single extra 27" (68.5 cm) to the total fabric amount, so that you can choose where the hem will be positioned.

Thus, 135" (343 cm) is needed for each cut; only 124½" (316 cm) is actually used for the curtain. The five 10½" (26.7 cm) pieces that are left can be used for tiebacks, cornices, cushions or a border for another window. Planning this carefully reduces waste and therefore cost.

PLANNING AND MEASURING SHADES

Once you have chosen the design of the shade and the position of the fittings, take accurate measurements to find the finished width and the overall drop. Final measurements can only be taken once the fittings are in place, but an estimate will enable you to order the correct amount of fabric.

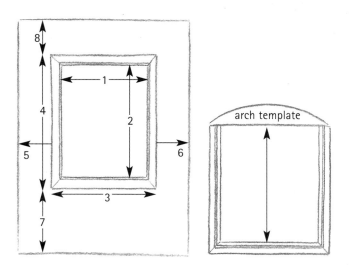

The following measurements are required:
1 Width of window frame
2 Height of window frame
3 Width of window reveal
4 Height of window reveal
5 Space to the left
6 Space to the right
7 Space below the sill
8 Space above the reveal

All shades need to be raised and lowered without interruption, so must be made exactly square. Very few windows have four corners at absolute right angles, so use a set square or level to determine the top line. Lightly pencil the top line on the frame or wall from which the measurements will be taken and to which the batten will be fitted. Measure both the width and the drop at 8" (20.5 cm) intervals. The narrowest or shortest measurement is the one which you must use to be sure that the shade can be raised and lowered without trouble. Where walls and plastering are uneven, you may need to take a line and work to it regardless of the window.

Most shades can be made to fit windows with shaped tops, the easiest are those with a fairly shallow curve. The shade will only pull up to the bottom of the curve, so some of the available light will be blocked. Mark a horizontal line as near to the bottom of the arched shape as possible. Cut a paper template of this arch, above this line. Measure from this line to where you wish the shade to finish.

To assess the length of fabric for cascade or Austrian shades, pin a length of string to the window from top of shade to hem position. Remove the string and measure, then add the length of each swag to find the fabric total.

ESTIMATING SHADE FABRIC

Each style of shade requires a different quantity of fabric. A rolled shade needs more length than a Roman shade. Use this example to estimate the amount of fabric needed for Roman shades.

1 To find the cut width

measure the batten	36" (91.5 cm)
add side hems 2 × 2" (5 cm)	4" (10 cm)
total	40" (102 cm)

2 To find the cut length

top to bottom	45" (115 cm)
add mounting allowance	1" (2.5 cm)
add for hem	4" (10 cm)
total	50" (127 cm)

Roman shades look best when the fabric is not interrupted by seams, so they are most suitable for windows that are at least 4" (10 cm) narrower than the fabric width. For wider windows, choose a shade style that camouflages seams. If vertical seams are necessary, place one full width of fabric in the center and flank each side with an equal-width partial panel.

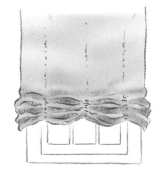

Cascade   Roman

London

Austrian

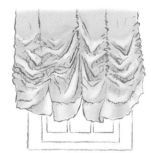

Festoon

Shade fittings

Roller shade kits include a roller and fixing brackets. Make sure that you follow the manufacturer's instructions when assembling the shade.

Rolled shades will fit to a batten with attached tapes, cords or ribbons to raise and lower them.

Cascade, Roman, London, Austrian and festoon shades all depend on the pulley system of a series of cords threaded through rings at regular intervals across the shade to operate them. Systems can be bought from curtain track suppliers. Or you can make a fabric-covered wooden batten to take the cord runners.

CURTAIN FITTINGS

Tracks

Metal tracks with plastic runners and an enclosed pull-cord system are the best for most uses. Buy to suit the

weight and length of your curtains. The fittings will be easily adaptable to top-fit onto a cornice board or into the recess, or to face-fit the wall or directly onto the window frame. Choose double or triple fittings where your layered design needs more than one track or a track/pole combination.

Extendable track

Some are available in kits which can be adjusted to fit a range of sizes. Useful for all windows, but especially if you move house often.

Tension rod

A sprung rod, good for lightweight curtains, which will fit snugly into a recess, the side walls holding it in place.

Slim tracks

Very fine metal tracks are available which fit onto wall or ceiling, to hold lightweight curtains or flat panels. Ideal for fitting behind a pole or double fittings for the under layer. Fitted towards the top, they are invisible from the front.

Crane rods

For door curtains and recesses, a single pole slips into a wall bracket and swings back against the side wall to open.

Cording

Cording to open and close curtains protects the edges of all curtains, especially those in light-colored fabric. Even the natural oil of the hand will cause a build-up of grime on the curtain edge in time. Cords may be worked on a continuous loop or with weights, depending on the size of your window. For wide windows consider an electrically operated system.

Track covers

Tracks and fittings are best unseen, so make a track cover in the same fabric as the curtains, then paper or paint it.

Cornice boards

Cornice boards need to suit the quality and weight of the curtaining and top treatments. Paint the board to match the window frame or cover the whole board with fabric to match the curtains.

Curtain poles

There are so many different types of pole and finial style available that you will be spoiled for choice. Choose poles that can be fitted as close to the wall as possible, with brackets that have fixings above and below the pole,

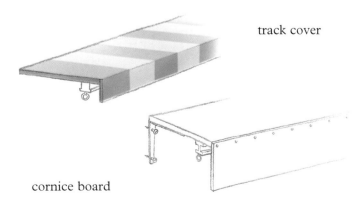

track cover

cornice board

otherwise heavy curtains could pull the fitting away from the wall. The end brackets should be positioned so that there is approximately 1" (2.5 cm) from the fitting to the end of the pole, just enough space for one curtain ring. The curtain will then pull right to the end of the pole.

From the plainest black metal to the most elaborately carved and gilded wood, the choice of pole is as essential to the overall design as the color, weight and fullness of the curtains. Fashions change and availability with them, but at the moment metal poles are in vogue. They are good for cottage windows or wherever space is limited and the fitting needs to be unobtrusive. Any rustic window or country-style room will benefit from narrow poles and interesting finials. They are always available in black, but can be over-painted with spray paints covered with a water-based varnish to protect the finish or with a brush and metal paint if you prefer not to use a spray. Seek out brass poles for a classic treatment, or wooden poles with finials from the simplest balls to the most elaborately carved designs from specialty suppliers.

Poles sleeved in hand-stitched leather are a luxurious option for the right room. Glass and acrylic poles look fantastic with lightweight curtains. If you really want to go all out, combine glass poles with the best silk taffeta for a light, contemporary look.

Special fittings

You might need to have fittings especially made for your window. There are specialty curtains fittings suppliers who will undertake almost anything, available through interior designers. In most areas you should be able to find a metal fabrication company who can take on even the most difficult window shapes, curtain frames and multiple fittings.

DRESSING CURTAINS

Formal styles

Hand-headed curtains need to be dressed as soon as they are hung so that the pleats are trained to fall evenly. You will need to leave the curtains tied back for at least 48 hours and possibly up to 96 hours. The waiting will be well rewarded, as your curtains will always hang well thereafter. Springy fabrics may need to be readjusted several times, but this will become easier as the pleats are trained.

1 Draw the curtains to the stack-back position.
2 Stand with the headings at eye level and arrange the pleats. The pleats are arranged forwards and the gaps (the fabric in between the pleats) folded evenly between each pleat. If the curtain hangs under a track or pole, fold the gaps behind the fitting; if in front, fold them to the front.
3 Take each pleat from the top and smooth it down the curtain as far as you can reach to form a fold. Follow these pleats through to waist height.
4 From the leading edge, fold each pleat back onto the last. Tie a strip of fabric loosely around the curtain to hold the pleats in place.
5 Kneel on the floor and follow the folds down to the hem. Finger press them into place firmly and tie another strip of fabric around to hold the pleats lightly.

Informal styles

If you want your new curtains to fall into soft folds, or to look as though they have been there for a long time, try one of the following window dressing ideas. Either pull the curtains back and forth about a hundred times to unstiffen the fabric, or pick them up, pull them towards you and drop them down again, until they have settled in nicely.

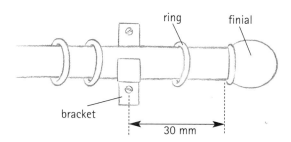

positioning of bracket

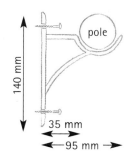

CURTAIN CARE

Regular care and attention will prevent curtains from becoming dirty. If disaster strikes, if someone in your household smokes or you light open fires, or if you are moving house and want to make alterations, use a dry cleaner known to you, or a furnishings specialist who will come and clean them in situ.

Washing

Unlined curtains are often made for situations where regular cleaning is necessary. If frequent washing is essential, use a strong, hardwearing fabric, such as cotton, with enough substance to stand regular handling.

Check the washing label attached and test a small off-cut of the same fabric. Measure and cut an exact square, wash, press and remeasure. If there is shrinkage which hasn't been allowed for, then either wash at a very low temperature, or dry clean.

Sunlight can react with the residue of cleaning chemicals and cause fading, so make sure fabrics are rinsed thoroughly. Always press when still damp, as pressing and steaming will keep the fabric in shape. Try not to press over seams; only press up to them with the point of the iron. If you do need to press over a seam, slip a piece of cloth between the seam and the main fabric to prevent a ridge from forming at the front of the curtain.

Dry cleaning

This is the only realistic option for interlined curtains, or for any curtains where more than one texture has been used. But generally, unless accident or smoke makes cleaning inevitable, dry cleaning should be avoided in favor of regular vacuuming and airing.

Airing

The best and most effective way to keep curtains clean and fresh is to choose a slightly breezy day, open the windows wide, close the curtains and allow them to blow in the breeze for a few hours. This will remove the slightly musty lining smell. If you can do this every few weeks, your curtains will always stay fresh. This is more of a problem in the city, but is possible if you choose quiet, breezy, sunny spring and autumn days.

Vacuuming

The regular removal of dust is vital to prevent particles of household dust settling into the fabric grain, as once dirt has penetrated, it is very difficult and often impossible to remove satisfactorily. Vacuum all soft furnishings regularly with a soft brush, paying special attention to the inside of chair seats, pleats and frills. For delicate fabrics and cornices, make a muslin or fine calico mob cap, elasticized to fit over the end of the brush, to soften the bristles and minimize fabric abrasion.

Alterations

If curtains need to be altered for any reason (such as when you move house), have them cleaned by a specialty dry cleaner before alterations are carried out. Remove stitching from the sides and hems first to allow any ruckled fabric to be cleaned and to allow the fabrics of curtain and lining to shrink to different degrees.

Track maintenance

Periodically spray the inside of the curtain track and top of the poles with an anti-static household cleaner or silicone spray to prevent dust building up and to ease their running. Poles may be cleaned with a dilute household cleaner and a soft brush to remove dust from the crevices of decorative finials and the underside of the rings.

Fire-proofing

Some fabrics are required by law to be fire-retardant, either as part of the weave or by a subsequent treatment of the fabric. If you are making curtains for a hotel, sports club, holiday accommodation or for any commercial building, you must check the current regulations and your supplier to make sure that the fabric you have chosen will pass the relevant tests. Many fabric companies produce special ranges that comply.

GLOSSARY

Acrylic: Manmade from petroleum, often mixed with more expensive fibers to keep the cost down. Not hard-wearing, but useful for permanent pleating.

Brocade: Traditionally woven fabric using silk, cotton, wool or mixed fibers, on a jacquard loom, in a multi- or self-colored floral design. Brocades drape well and so are good for heavy curtains. Some are washable but most will need dry cleaning.

Cambric: Closely woven, plain weave fabric from linen or cotton with a sheen on one side. Use, wash and press as calico. Widely used for cushion pads but also for curtains.

Canvas: Plain weave cottons in various weights suitable for inexpensive curtains. Available as unbleached, coarse cotton or more finely woven and dyed in strong colors.

Challis: A soft lightweight fabric in slightly open plain weave with soft handle, similar to voile. May be plain or printed wool or cotton.

Chintz: Cotton fabric in plain colors or printed designs with a resin finish which gives a characteristic sheen or glaze and which also repels dirt. The glaze will eventually wash out, so only dry clean curtains. Avoid using steam to press and never fold as the glaze will crack.

Corduroy: A strong fabric woven to form vertical ridges by floating extra yarn across, which is then cut to make the pile. Press on a velvet pinboard while damp.

Cotton: A natural fiber, it is very versatile, woven, knitted and mixed with other fibers. Use for any drapery according to weight. It will lose strength in direct sunlight, so protect. Soft, strong, washable if preshrunk.

Crewel: Plain or hopsack woven, natural cotton background embroidered in chainstitch in cream or multicolored wools. Soft but heavy, lovely for curtains and soft shades. May be washed but test a small piece first.

Damask: A jacquard fabric first woven in Damascus with satin floats on a warp satin background in cotton, silk, wool and mixed fibers in various weights. Use for curtains and drapes, choosing different weights for different uses. Make up reversed if a matte finish is required. Suitable for curtaining which will be seen from both sides.

Dead light: This refers to the area between the top of a window and the ceiling where any light entering the room is insignificant and sometimes distracting.

Gingham: Plain weave fabric in 100% cotton with equal width stripes of white and one other color in warp and weft threads to create checks or stripes. For small windows in cottagey rooms, kitchens and children's bedrooms. Mix with floral patterns and other checks and stripes.

Habutai: The term means "soft and light" and was originally used for Japanese waste silk. It is now made in many Far Eastern countries on power looms in plain or twill weave. It is heavier than traditional Chinese silk and is usually in natural ecru color. Also sometimes used to describe a very fine lightweight silk, dyed in many colors.

Holland: Firm, hard-wearing fabric made from cotton or linen stiffened with oil or shellac. Use for shades, curtaining and cornices.

Lace: Open-work fabrics in designs ranging from simple spots to elaborate panels. Usually in cotton or in a cotton and polyester mixture.

Lawn: A very smooth fabric. It is lighter in weight than cambric, may be plain or printed, and has a slightly stiff finish which may be permanent. It is a plain weave fabric made from cotton or linen and is very cool, absorbent and hard-wearing.

Linen: Fibers found inside the stalks of the flax plant are woven to make linen cloth in almost any weight. Distinctive slub weave, from very fine linen for under-curtains and sheers to heavy upholstery weight. A very strong fiber which is easy to work.

Moiré: A finish usually on silk or acetate described as watermarked. The characteristic moiré markings are produced by pressing plain woven fabric through hot engraved cylinders which crush the threads and push them into different directions to form the pattern. The finish will disappear on contact with water.

Muslin: Coarse, plain weave cotton in cream or white with natural flecks in it. Available in many widths and weights for inexpensive curtains. Wash before use to shrink and press while damp.

Organdy: The very finest cotton fabric with an acid finish giving it a unique crispness. Use for lightweight curtains. Wash and press while damp.

Organza: Similar to organdy and made of silk, polyester or viscose. Very springy and used for stiffening headings of fine fabrics, shades to filter sunlight and to protect curtains. Use layers of varying tones together.

Provençal prints: Fine cotton with small printed designs in bright colors. Originally Indian designs, now mostly printed in Provence. Washable, hard-wearing, the best hardly crease.

Reveal: Literally, to "reveal a view". Here, the sides of the hole in the wall in which the window fits.

Scrim: White or off-white, inexpensive, open-weave cloth which can be dyed in pastel colors. Use for under-curtains and sheers in hot countries to filter light and insects.

Sheers: Fabrics which are thin enough to let light through, such as scrims and voiles. The primary use for sheer fabrics is to provide privacy while letting in more or less light, depending on their weave and design. They were traditionally used behind heavy curtains but interior designers are increasingly using sheers as the main fabric. When not required to provide extra insulation, sheers create a delightful light, airy effect.

Silk: From the cocoon of the silk worm, silk is soft and luxurious to touch. Fades in sunlight, so protect. Available in every weight, from lamp shade to heavy upholstery. Good mixed with cotton or wool.

Silk voile: Light to medium weight silk, relatively inexpensive for curtaining. Not a great range of colors, but the natural slub and matte finish are attractive.

Silk shantung: Light silk woven with irregular yarns giving a dull sheen. Use to line bed curtains, as under-curtains where protected from sunlight. Shantung gathers and frills easily and drapes well. Use lots of fullness. Available in a huge range of colors.

Stackback: The wall area at the side of the window covered by the curtain. The curtain 'stacks back' or folds into this area when opened.

Taffeta: The best is 100% silk but can be woven from acetate and blends. Acetates are most useful where the look of silk is wanted without the risk of rotting or fading.

Tartan: Authentic plaids belong to individual Scottish clans and are woven in fine wool twill, originally for kilts. Available in several weights. Use the heaviest for thick curtains and the finest for light. The fabric is the same on both sides, so use for doorways and unlined curtains.

Ticking: Traditional cotton herringbone weave in black and white used for mattresses and pillow covers. Very dense weave and good for inexpensive, stylish curtains.

Toile de Jouy: Pastoral designs in single color tones on a white or sometimes colored ground; the best designs are engraved copper plate and hand-printed.

Tweed: Wool worsted cloth in dogstooth check and muted stripes and checks. Mainly from Scotland and Ireland, the suiting quality is hard-wearing yet drapes very well. Good for curtains, especially for country use.

Velvet: Available in cotton, wool, linen and silk. The fine pile throws the light and the cloth looks a much lighter color upside down. Careful stitching is needed so that fabrics don't walk on each other as the opposite piles meet. Pull a small piece of the cloth to test the quality. If threads pull out easily the cloth won't stand even one cleaning without weakening.

Viscose: Wood pulp woven into fibers which mixes well with other fibers helping them to take dyes and fireproofing. Washable and sheds dirt easily.

Voile: Fine lightweight cotton or linen or wool. Any color available. Use for fine curtains, bed curtains and drapes. Choose one which will wash and dry easily. Good polyester voile looks just like cotton, is usually fireproof and will wash and dry like a dream.

Wool: A natural fiber, liable to excessive shrinkage as the scales on each fiber overlap, harden and felt. Is warm to touch and initially resists damp.

INDEX

ACKNOWLEDGEMENTS

By its very nature a portfolio represents the ideas and notes amassed by one person over a period of time, so much credit goes to all those who have at any time influenced design in general, and the craft of curtain–making in particular, and to the magazines which have published them. Other ideas are solutions in response to problems or evolve from the continual search for the next idea and for these I am indebted to those for whom we have made curtains.

   More specifically, my thanks to Rowan Suenson–Taylor for translating my jottings into readable sketches and for the overall design concept. To Lisa for typing the main text and to Rosemary, Steve and Sara for their skills in turning this raw material into a cohesive book.